The Real
High School Handbook

The Real
High School Handbook

———— A ————

*How to Survive, Thrive, and
Prepare for What's Next*

Susan Abel Lieberman, Ph.D.

A Mariner Original
Houghton Mifflin Company
Boston • New York
1997

For information about permission to reproduce selections from
this book, write to Permissions, Houghton Mifflin Company,
215 Park Avenue South, New York, New York 10003.

Library of Congress Cataloging-in-Publication Data

Lieberman, Susan Abel.
The real high school handbook : how to survive, thrive, and prepare
for what's next / Susan Abel Lieberman.
p.   cm.
"A Mariner Original."
Includes index.
Summary: A guide to getting through high school and deciding what
will come next, providing information about courses, grades,
testing, communicating with teachers, and postgraduation options.
ISBN 0-395-79760-8
1. High schools — United States — Handbooks, manuals, etc. —
Juvenile literature. 2. High school students — United States —
Conduct of life — Handbooks, manuals, etc. — Juvenile literature.
[1. High schools. 2. Schools.]   I. Title.
LB1620.5.L53   1997
373.18'0973 — dc21   97-26558 CIP AC

Book design by Joyce Weston
Printed in the United States of America

QUM 10 9 8 7 6 5 4 3 2 1

For orders of 5,000 copies or more, this book can be customized
with information specific to state and local school districts. For
more information on how to order a custom edition, please write to
Houghton Mifflin Company, Trade and Reference Division Special
Sales Department, Attn: The Real High School Handbook Custom
Edition, 222 Berkeley Street, Boston, Massachusetts 02116.

Contents

Acknowledgments

The African saying that it takes a whole village to raise a child has been used so much in this country that it now seems American. The message certainly feels right for our time, and this book is all about using the resources of the village to enrich the high school years. But if it takes a village to raise a child, it also takes a village to write a book like this for teens.

So many people have contributed to this project in important ways, and to all of them, I am grateful. I could never have done this work without their assistance. A few made such significant contributions that I want to honor them publicly.

The Houston Independent School Board planted the seeds for this national edition when it unanimously approved the funds to publish a localized edition for all Houston Independent School District (HISD) eighth to twelfth graders. I am especially grateful to the 1995 board, to Dr. Rod Paige, HISD superintendent, Dr. Susan Sclafani, Chief of Staff and, most especially, Rosalind Young, Associate Superintendent for Communications and Public Affairs, for their vision, leadership, and trust.

Betty Porter, the head counselor at Milby High School in Houston, Texas, arranged for me to meet with a group of students on a regular basis and then read the Houston draft and reviewed her comments page by page. This was an extraordinary gift of time that was enriched by her enthusiasm for the project and her loving insights about teens.

Sue Reynolds carefully read every word of the draft for this edition and, via lengthy e-mail messages, gave me terrific advice and a deeper understanding of the issues high school counselors as well as high school students face. Ms. Reynolds is a past vice president for secondary schools for the American Counselor Association and the 1994 counselor of the year. She was certainly counselor of the year for me in 1996.

Dr. Kenneth Hoyt, at the School of Education, Kansas State University, was especially generous in sharing labor force and school-to-work data. Even more helpful than the data was his gentle tutelage in the career issues facing students today. Dr. Robert Glover at the University of Texas at Austin's Center for the Study of Human Resources has been a good friend over several books and contributed in the same subject area.

The Houston book and this one were developed and written under the auspices of Super Summers, Inc., a nonprofit organization founded in 1994 to distribute accessible, accurate information to teens. I may have put the wheels in motion, but Antonia Day, Robert Frank, Laurence Payne, and Rosalind Young, the founding board members, and Jody Blazek, our accountant, keep the show on the road. They are mentors, advisors, critics and, sometimes, therapists. I am in their debt. My agent, Barrie Van Dyck, plays a similar role. For her good sense and her good friendship, I am grateful. I am grateful, too, to Marnie Patterson Cochran, my editor at Houghton Mifflin, for her red pencil.

The first young woman I mentored, Stephanie Hickerson, was so determined, so hungry to advance, so satisfying to see flourish that she hooked me on working with high school students. Now Stephanie Hickerson Harris, an honors graduate of Spelman College and a graduate of the University of Louisville School of Law, she taught me far more than I ever taught her, and I owe her a great debt. Cindy, Lisa, Junior V and Junior A, Carlos, Winnetka, Samantha, Linece, Maria, and Olga all were my teachers in learning about the issues high school students must address. I hope I have touched their lives. I know they touched mine.

If our sons Seth and Jonathan had not decided to be productive and enjoyable young men, I doubt that I would have had the courage to write about teens at all. I know I would not have been able to do this work without my husband Michael's steady support and affection. When the work takes longer and seems harder than imagined, family and friends are what keep me from sending my cranky muse packing, and I thank them all — including the muse.

1. Master of Your Fate, Captain of Your Soul

What Is This Book About?

The Real High School Handbook is about *how to survive and thrive* in high school. It is about your having the information you need when you need it. Most of all, it is about *you* being in control of *your* life.

While working on this book, I met with students from time to time, mostly juniors and seniors, in a psychology class at Milby High School in Houston. These students provided valuable feedback and advice. Asked, "What would *you* write to students?" one senior answered:

> I wish I could go back and start over again. All you think about is that you want to fit in with the crowd because you are new. So you skip class, don't do class work or homework, do what everybody else is doing . . . Now it's my turn to tell what I wish I had heard. "Do things for yourself, not for anybody else. You won't get anywhere if you do things just to fit in with others. There will be a lot of regrets and a lot of what-ifs in your life if you don't take the advice of someone who knows from experience.

A guy in the back of the class shouted, "I would write the *true* stuff, not all the things that we believe that aren't really true."

And a freshman at Yale University said, "I would tell students there is more to understand than grades. Learning balance in high school helps you in college."

Read this book and you won't be saying *"if only . . ."* when you're a senior. Here is "true stuff" you need to know to get the most out of high school. If you are already a senior, here's last-minute help with some of the decisions facing you. If you are an eighth or ninth grader, it's your good fortune to have the true stuff before you begin.

> Tell them that this book answers lots of questions you want to ask but are afraid you will be laughed at for asking.
> —*Milby High School senior*

> I wish somebody would have told me that as long as I believe in myself, it will turn out O.K." —*Milby High School junior*

I spent hundreds of hours talking with high school students, listening to their problems, hearing them explain how they got into and out of jams, what confused them, and what helped them to succeed. With all of these conversations in mind, here is what I would say if you and I could sit down at your kitchen table to talk:

- Every day is a fresh start — regardless of what happened to you yesterday or last year. You and only you decide whether you will be happy, sad, mad, in charge or out of control. Why not choose things to help yourself rather than hurt yourself?

- You get one chance to go through this life; the choices you make determine how your story turns out. You are your own script writer, but you can't go back and rewrite what has already happened.

- It doesn't matter whether your family is educated or not, rich or poor, supportive or difficult, or whether your teachers are fabulous or cranky; you still get to decide every day at school — regardless of what anyone else does — what you are going to do with your head and your heart.

- Just wishing for success isn't enough. You must believe, deep inside, that your success is desirable and possible. Then you will be able to make the hard choices that success sometimes requires.

Just What Is High School About? High school is not simply an idea adults cooked up to keep teenagers off the streets and out of the house. You are laying the foundation for your adult life. If you were building a house to live in for the rest of your life, would you use second-rate materials, cut corners on the workmanship or ignore the building instructions? If you did, it is a pretty sure bet that later on you'd be envious of your neighbors living in houses with fewer problems and better looks.

Many students struggle in high school because they are unsure just why they are there and why they should be working in their classes. Teenagers are not dumb and, like adults, generally act in a way that reflects what they believe is good for them. As with adults, however, their beliefs can be out of focus.

As a fourteen-year-old or an eighteen-year-old, you still have so much to experience in the world. Because so much has happened to you from childhood to now, it may feel like you must have learned most of what there is to know. Feeling this way, it is easy to miss huge pieces of information that don't feel important now but become important later. Think of being a little kid and going to a crowded parade. Maybe you wiggled your way to the front and, between the legs of the adults, you could see the parade going by in front of you. The view was excellent. You got a perfect look at what happened just as it passed by you, but you could not see what was coming or what happened after it passed you until an adult lifted you up on his shoulders, and your view of the parade got much larger. Perhaps what was happening in front of you became less important because you were looking at a bigger picture with lots more to see. This same shift in perspective can help with school. Look at high school from the air not the ground.

The Foundation for the Rest of Your Life Far more important than any one specific school subject is your ability to take hold of your situation and make it work to your advantage. If you can do it in high school, you will probably do it after high school. If you blow high school, the game is not over, but everything else that comes after is tougher. **High**

school is your first serious test to determine how well you are going to do in managing your own life.

Every class you take in high school gives you the chance to learn how to learn, how to follow through, how to figure out what you don't understand. Those classes, regardless of whether they are in math, music, or mechanics, are intended to develop your ability to uncover information and manage time and resources in a world of rules and regulations. They are meant to teach you how to look intelligently at ideas and facts and then define your own interests and values. They also help you develop your ability to get along with all kinds of people.

Relationships are especially important to teenagers, and that's good because success in the world is far more likely to be determined by your ability to forge healthy relationships than by grades. But when you are focusing on relationships, don't be narrow-minded. It's not just how you relate to a few friends; it's how you relate to everybody. If the people you relate well to are headed straight toward trouble or boredom or cynicism, maybe you want to think about what it would be like also to have relationships with people who are headed for success, who are engaged and excited by ideas and positive opportunities. If you are relating poorly toward teachers or adult authority figures, think about what is going on with you that makes these relationships difficult. Is it always the "other guy's" fault? Develop an effective way to handle difficult people or difficult situations and you will have a skill that will serve you well for a lifetime.

All You Can Control Is You Yes, of course, what is going on in your family, in your neighborhood, and in your life affect how you feel and act. But there's no use in blaming other people for what is happening because it is unlikely you can change them. The star center on the opposing basketball team might be taller, faster or meaner, but if you are in the middle of the game, you can't worry about how to make this guy shorter, slower or nicer. You have to focus on what YOU can do to win the game. If home is a hard place to be just now, talk with your parents about your getting involved in activities that will get you out of the house in a productive way.

How Do You Use This Book?

You can read this book straight through if you want to, but there is another way. Skim it. Check out the Table of Contents and the Index. Get a sense of all that is in the book. Then use it like a cookbook. Go to different sections as you need them. Start anywhere and read what interests you at the moment. Leave your book by the kitchen table, in the family room, or beside your bed. Pick it up now and then and read a bit here and there. Make notes in the margins. Underline information you think you will want to find again. You can even tear out a page and tape it to the wall if you want to be reminded of it regularly.

With more than 20,000 high schools in the United States, it is impossible to provide complete details for every situation, but this book will help you to ask the right questions and understand high school policies and procedures for your district. Share the book with friends, but don't let them walk off with your copy. Let this book be yours, notated and marked just for your needs. Keep it around so you have the information you need when you need it.

High school is your first serious test to determine how well you are going to manage the rest of your life. Much more important than any specific high school subject is your ability to take control of a situation and make it work to your advantage. If you can do this in high school, you will probably continue to do it after high school. If you blow high school, everything else that follows will be tougher.

All of the required subjects give you the chance to learn:

- how to follow through
- how to figure out what you don't understand
- how to learn

Your courses develop your ability to:

- uncover needed information
- manage time and resources in a world of rules and regulations

School aims to:

- prepare you to look intelligently at ideas and facts
- define your own interests and values

Learn these lessons and you will be ready to walk out the door of high school and organize a life for yourself. The school district cannot make high school work *for* you. It can only work *with* you.

2. What Attitude Are You Wearing?

How Is School Like Sports?

Think of your favorite sports team. Who is the coach? Now why does the team owner waste money hiring this coach when the players already are experts at their game? When I put this question to high school students, they look at me like I am not too bright. "What do you mean, 'Why do we have a coach?'" one muscly young man scoffed. "Have you ever heard of a winning team without a coach?"

No, I haven't. Athletes, of course, need coaches who

- help them figure out how to get better
- make sure they do the drills they need to stay in shape
- look for ways to stretch their players
- play mind games to bring out players' best attitudes

Who Is Your Coach? Without an academic coach on the sidelines, lots of students don't know how to run their own practice sessions. They forget that victory is possible. They don't study well; maybe they don't study at all.

You must be the outstanding captain of your own team. You have got to give yourself that winning attitude. If you know anything about sports, you already know that attitude is more important than built-in ability. Your teachers, counselors and parents are a crew of coaches. Homework is the drills. Class is the practice session. You are the star.

Your teachers are ready to pour information into and pull understanding out of you. In order to teach you, however, you have to be like the athlete who is prepared to get out on the field and compete. If you are not putting out learning energy, it is not fair to complain about the teacher's teaching energy.

You won't like every teacher, and every teacher won't like you. That's just life. There are unfair teachers, but most teachers are fair even if you do not like their rules of fairness. Stop thinking about the teacher liking you or you liking the teacher. Think about this:

- How can I learn in this class?
- What information does this teacher have to offer me that I need to know?
- What can I do to turn this class into a positive experience?

What About Criticism? Nobody enjoys criticism — neither teens nor teachers. Some people are better about correcting in a way that doesn't hurt your feelings, and others are not good at it at all. Remember that criticism about your work is not criticism about who you are as a person. If you write a lousy English essay you are not a lousy person, but you may have done third-rate work for this moment — and you need to hear it and use that to figure out how to write a better essay.

Teachers Are Human Beings Now and then, put yourself in the shoes of your teachers. I have heard teachers talking in the teachers' lounge who sound like maybe they dislike teens. And then I see those very same teachers spending extra time with students, working hard on their lessons and feeling good when a student succeeds. It seems to me that what teachers dislike is watching students they know can do well making hurtful choices. They dislike spending all day trying to teach material they believe with all their hearts will help you only to find that you are not even trying to learn. It makes them grumpy and bad-spirited. In the worst situations, it makes them give up.

Some students have "an attitude." Maybe you have one? It's the

"You can't tell me what to do. I am my own person and that doesn't have anything to do with you" approach to the world. You *are* your own person. But don't belittle a teacher. Imagine the situation reversed. Behave the way you want to be treated. For the most part, let your teachers be who they are — terrific or not so terrific. Remember, everything that is going on is not about you. Often, a teacher's behavior is a window on what has been going on for the teacher. Take the knowledge your teachers have to offer. Offer them some of your knowledge in return. If you like them, so much the better. If you don't, be polite. Ignore what you can and concentrate on making a difficult situation work. You will be moving on in no time.

Teaching Is a Dance

Compare you and your teachers to dance partners. In dancing, if one partner is wooden and stiff, limp and heavy, or unwilling to get out of the chair and onto the dance floor, the other partner can't dance well, if at all. Teachers should be the most graceful and fluid teachers they can be. But you, the student, must also be flexible and ready. Students contribute a great deal to the atmosphere in the classroom. Like dancing, when students gracefully follow the teacher's lead and gently signal their own needs, learning is more interesting and enjoyable for everybody.

When you sleep in class, it may be because you are tired, but think about how you'd feel if you were in front of the room trying to explain something difficult to a person who could not stay awake — or who was talking, passing notes, reading a book, or fixing makeup. Just as annoying are students who are able to grasp the material quickly and become impatient, sometimes, even arrogant. Important decisions about people usually are made as much on their personalities, behavior, and character as their intellectual abilities. Really smart people know that rudeness doesn't pay, and they adapt their dance style to suit the partners on hand.

Parents as Partners

Can you remember when you started riding a bike? Sometimes you went too fast and fell and your parents picked you up, hugged you, and sent you on your way again. Sometimes, they held your bike until you were steady enough to go it alone. One last time, let your parents play the same supporting role as you move toward being an independent adult. Let them give you their best advice and help you out. Don't wall them off from school or from your life. If they know your teachers and feel comfortable at your school, it will be easier for them to help you if problems at school do crop up. Talk with them about your thoughts, worries, and hopes. Lying to your parents doesn't make you clever. It makes you a liar.

Odds are that your parents worry a lot about you and want to make sure that you don't trip into trouble. Parents are not always very good at explaining their worry — and sometimes they worry needlessly. Often, teens aren't very good at understanding why parents worry. That can lead to conflict. If you are fighting with your parents, don't waste your energy. Most of these fights are really about power and control — about who's in charge of your life. Relax. You win! In the long run, you'll go out in the world and lead the life you choose. But for the next few years give your parents' judgment a chance. You will be on your own soon enough.

Most parents are doing the best they can. If your parents are really getting to you, take a minute to step back and think about what is going on. Why, you have got to ask yourself, are they doing or saying these things that annoy you? Nine times out of ten, if you are honest with yourself, you will see that their reasons make sense even if the way they carry them out doesn't work for you. Why, for example, do parents nag kids about homework? It isn't because parents enjoy nagging. It isn't because they like to make you irritated. And it isn't because they have nothing better to do. They want so much for you to do well in the world and have choices, and they worry that you won't be prepared to get what you want. Parents set rules about drinking, driving, dating, and talking on the phone to keep you safe and focused, to help you move forward successfully.

Of course, you may not want the help. Andrew, an eleventh grader, said, "I wish my parents would get off my back about homework. I'm working as hard as I can." But, when pushed, he admits that he is working as hard as he *wants* — not as hard as he can. When asked why he doesn't do a little more and get his grades up, he answers honestly, "I don't know."

In Andrew's house, the fight has shifted, without anyone realizing it, from how much time Andrew should spend on homework to who's in control of Andrew's life. In order to win the fight, Andrew has to insist that he's doing enough. It would make everyone feel better if Andrew could sit down with his parents and say, "Look, you're right. I do need to spend more time on school work, but I just can't seem to make myself concentrate. It seems so boring and unimportant and I just end up day-dreaming away." Maybe Andrew's parents can help if he lets them. Maybe they will just yell at him and tell him to stop being self-indulgent and do what he needs to do to get better grades. I can't promise you things will get better if you level with your parents, but when you decrease the conflict and increase the honest communication, the odds of things improving increase enormously.

Prejudice

An issue that sometimes gets between students and teachers or students and students is race. Race and prejudice are such difficult issues to talk about that people often avoid them or, if they must discuss them, speak in the most general, safest language. But when teens talk honestly about school, race issues come up all the time. Yes, there are teachers who have prejudices, and sometimes those prejudices show up in class. Yes, there are students who have prejudices, and sometimes their prejudices show up, too. But be careful that you are not imagining prejudice when the problem has nothing to do with race.

This story illustrates the point:

I had this English teacher, and he didn't like Hispanics, I thought. He was always picking on me and giving me bad grades and stuff, and I decided I wasn't going to bother with his class. But he wouldn't leave me alone. He kept picking on me — and making me work. After a while, I started talking with this guy more, and he kept telling me, "Junior, you are smart enough to do this work so stop being lazy and having this attitude and produce for me." Well, anyway, by the end of the year, I saw that it wasn't because he didn't like me. He was just annoyed because I didn't hand in my homework and was going to fail the class. I was wrong about him — and he was right about me.

If you think a teacher has racial or other prejudices because the teacher does or says things that make you uncomfortable, make an appointment to talk with this teacher. Say something like, "I want to talk with you about something that is making me very uncomfortable in class. This is hard to talk about, but I thought it would help both of us if I told you honestly how things look to me." Here's the trick: when you are explaining what bothers you, use sentences that start with "I" instead of "You." When you start an explanation with an accusative "you," the other person is likely to become defensive before you have even finished your explanation. For example, you might say, "I feel put down when you say such and such in class." This is a much more effective approach than starting the sentence with, "You always put me down . . ."

Sometimes the problem will be yours, sometimes, your teacher's. Understanding the values and expectations of different cultures can be difficult for teachers as well as students. But if a teacher gives you some disagreeable news, don't get mad at the teacher because you don't like the news. What is important is to move beyond naming problems to a situation where you can get comfortable learning in that class. That is *your* goal. Be in charge of figuring out how to make it happen.

In every high school there are tensions between different groups of students, and sometimes these tensions have to do with race. I have never met a student who liked these tensions and thought they were good for the school. But I have also met very few students who were willing to talk about them publicly, confront their friends, or refuse to listen to any insulting remarks about others. If students refused to act or think or talk prejudicially and insisted that these problems be discussed with the help of a skilled adult when they surfaced, students themselves could change the atmosphere of their schools.

Here is a way to check yourself. When you catch yourself thinking or making a racial statement about an individual or a group of kids — a statement like "Anglo kids always__" "It's the black kids who__" "The Hispanics are the ones that__" or "I think Asians are__" — imagine a person of a different race saying the same thing about your ethnic or religious group and decide if you would consider that prejudice. If you answer yes, clean up your act.

We live in an imperfect world filled with imperfect people. If you can do a few things to make that world better, to make yourself better, to make people understand one another more, then you are, in my mind, a hero. And there is lots of room for heroes of all races, sexes, sizes, and colors in this world.

Grade-Grubbing Grinds/Goal-Grubbing Halfbacks

Do you think of the students who do well at school as "grade-grubbing grinds," or do you fear that your own excellent performance will label you as some kind of nerd? If someone is gifted as an athlete, the whole school cheers. And if someone less gifted really works hard and shines on the sports field, the school cheers again. At the end of the year, your school might have a special assembly and give these people school letters to wear on their jackets. But if someone is intellectually gifted or spends time and effort working hard at academics that don't come easily, that person is likely to be teased with mean-spirited words like "grade-grubbing" or "grind." The star basketball player doesn't pass up a basket to avoid looking too showy, but high school students will lie about getting good grades in order not to seem "too successful." Does this strike you as weird?

Football players don't apologize for scoring touchdowns or wanting to win, and you should never apologize for wanting good grades or for getting them. Grades are how we keep score for academics — and since you must show up and play the game every day, why not play to win? Allow yourself the benefit of an attitude that says "Yes, grades matter. How I do matters. What I do matters. I am smart enough to know that an education will help me, and I care enough about myself to give myself what I need."

It's easier to make fun of someone with good grades than to get them yourself. But people with their brains in gear spend their energies pulling themselves up, not putting others down. Get your brain going; let it embrace the message that high school is for real, your life is for real, and now is the time to get it right. If your brain embraces this message, your body will follow by doing what it needs to do to make high school work for you.

3. For Ninth Graders Only

Lots of students feel so overwhelmed by moving from middle school to high school that all they can focus on is fitting in and figuring out how they are supposed to act. Don't be too quick to decide how you are going to handle this new place. Take it slowly.

You can try so hard to fit in with the crowd that you lose your true self — and when you do get in, sometimes you can't handle the pressure. Then kids start having trouble in school, and it just starts to steamroll all over the place. So, what I'm trying to say is that when you get to high school, don't try to expect so much. Just let it come to you; don't go to it. You have four years. You don't have to figure out the social scene in four weeks.

—Milby High School senior

I failed classes, and I know it's hard, but I want to tell students not to give up . . . hang in there and get through it . . . Sometimes before you get to high school, you watch TV about how high school life is with parties, having sex, staying out late, and just having fun. When you get to high school, it's totally different from what you saw on television. *—Milby High School senior*

When you get to high school, you don't know what to do. So you look around and see what other people are doing. You see kids acting crazy and doing wild stuff and everybody seems to look at them and like them so you think that's what you should do. It took me a whole year to figure out that what I really was supposed to be doing was studying because nobody ever talks about doing that.

—Westbury High School sophomore

I was so nervous about being at the top of my class and getting into a good college that I missed out on part of high school. I wish I had taken a class in car mechanics and gone to more football games and been more relaxed. Tell people that it doesn't really matter if you are at one of the Ivy Leagues, where I am, or one of the dozens of other really top schools. Everybody seems to be equally satisfied.

—*University of Pennsylvania sophomore*

I figured I would just pretend I knew what I was doing until I figured things out. I never talked in class. I didn't join anything because I couldn't figure out what to join or how to do it. I kind of disappeared in the crowd. And what happened is I never really figured much out, and now I think I wasted a lot of my time.

—*Milby High School senior*

Friendship

At two, you're learning to talk. At six, you're decoding reading. In your teens, you're developing greater independence. As you consider separating from your parents, you look to friends for understanding and for help figuring out who you are, where you are going, and how you are going to get there.

Yet most ninth graders feel a little shaky about finding friends. As a result, some people start putting down other people in order to feel "in." Teens form gangs or cliques to make them feel part of an important group. Girls look for guys so they can say, "Someone finds me attractive, and so I must be O.K." Guys are thinking about girls and want reassurance that "Yes, I'm an O.K. guy." Students who are not attracted to the opposite sex start worrying about who they are and what choices they want to make. *This is a tough time.* And there is no simple formula for telling you how to get through it well, but there is lots of research that shows us that teens who do certain things have more success, and teens who ignore warnings from friends and family eventually express regret.

Five Things You Can Do to Help Yourself in School

Here are five things you can do to give yourself a better chance of doing well in high school:

1. **Pick friends who will help you graduate.** We behave like the people we spend time with. Hang around with people who cut school, have no plans for the future, and are likely to drop out, and you immediately increase the odds that you will drop out. Pick for friends people who are going somewhere more interesting than the corner store. If you have trouble making these kinds of friendships, try to find out what it is that keeps them at a distance.

2. **Be kind to your lungs and your liver.** Students who drink and/or smoke put themselves at risk to do less well in school. Maybe it's because these choices reflect bad judgment in general. Maybe it's because they indicate too much of a concern with how you look to others. Research does not yet indicate the reason, but there is a link between smoking, drinking, and lower school performance.

   For generations, teenagers have associated smoking and drinking with feeling grown up. In the last few decades, drinking and smoking have also become closely associated with death, sickness, and disability. We now understand that alcohol and nicotine are addicting drugs, and, frankly, you are nuts to start in on either one. If you never start, you will never have to struggle with how to stop. It is far more grown up to be kind to your lungs and your liver than lean against the wall with a beer or a cigarette. If you have already started smoking or drinking, find a program that can help you stop. It will only get harder to stop later on.

continued on next page

3. **Find a non-chemical way to handle stress.** You already know that getting involved with drugs is a road to trouble. Do whatever you have to do to avoid getting sucked into drugs. Stay away from people that you know do drugs. If pushed, say "That stuff is way too scary for me." Don't believe that a little bit of this or that can help you handle stress. Doing drugs is illegal, and breaking the law can lead you into big-time troubles with super stress. If you don't learn to handle stress without drugs now, you will not be prepared for your life after high school. Find a technique that works for you — whether it's taking a walk, doing deep breathing, spending five minutes on relaxation meditation, or dancing to the radio. Exercise, sports, music, dance, and meditation are all better ways to manage stress than drugs and drink. Laughter is one of the best stress relievers.

4. **Turn off the tube.** Students who watch more than three hours of television a day put themselves at higher risk for failure. Turn it off. Instead, get involved in activities that put you at risk to succeed. Studies show that teens who volunteer and/or who are active in organized sports, singing, arts, or other school activities at least one hour a week give themselves an added advantage for success. Find something at school or in the community that appeals to you and get involved. It will take time to feel part of the group, but if you begin in ninth grade, you can have four years of benefits.

5. **Find helpful adults.** Find caring adults outside your immediate family to have as friends. Students who have responsible adults, in addition to parents, to support them, listen to them, and talk with them regularly do better in school. A good place to find such adults is by getting involved in religious, scouting, community, or volunteer programs.

Carla was starting her senior year at Madison High in Claremont, California, when I asked her what she would say to ninth graders. She replied:

Oh, that's hard because I know I didn't want to listen to what anybody told me. I just wanted to have fun — and did have fun, but now I am really suffering. I didn't think it mattered how I did in ninth grade. I wrote letters in class. I cut class. I didn't do my homework. When you do these things for awhile it's like an addiction. When you want to change later, it is really hard . . . But I don't know what you could say that would make a ninth grader listen. Who wants to believe they are going to suffer, they are going to fail? They are going to regret having fun.

Parent Involvement Keep your parents in the loop. Parents can make the mistake of thinking that once teens are in high school, they are old enough to make all their own decisions and fight their own battles; teens can make the mistake of thinking they are too old to ask advice or tell parents about school. It is still helpful to have adults around as a sounding board. You already know that parents see things differently. But different can be useful.

You benefit when the adults in your life come to open house and other school events or volunteer at your school. It helps to have your family and your teachers and counselors know each other. Informally solving problems that pop up can be much easier than dealing with them formally. If you can't convince a family member to put a foot inside your school, ask your counselor if there is any chance of finding a mentor who can help you with course planning and come to school when an adult is needed. The more resources you have in this world, the better off you are. Helpful adults are a great resource.

Filling in the Academic Holes

The first chapter of this book talks about using high school to build a foundation strong enough to support a successful adult life. But what if the foundation you were supposed to get in grade school and/or middle school has cracks and holes? What if you didn't learn the pieces you

The Blank Look

You know the look. A student is sitting at his desk, looking ahead, but there is no life in his eyes. He is not engaged in the classroom at all. Or she is staring off somewhere, clearly in a different world.

It's discouraging for an instructor to try to teach in a way that's interesting and understandable and see blank faces giving no feedback, showing no interest. The blank look contributes to bad teaching. Good teaching makes it harder for kids to go blank, but no matter how wonderful a teacher, he or she cannot always fight off the energy-sucking effects of blankness.

Students go blank when they are angry, tired, depressed, or confused. They also go blank when they decide there is no reason for them to be where they are, when what is happening in the classroom doesn't seem to matter to them. Do whatever it takes in life to avoid blankness. It is unhealthy and unhappy, and, worse, it takes you nowhere.

need to make high school work? You have two choices: 1) Ignore the problem. Pretend you will get by. Meet failure in high school and, perhaps, drop out. 2) Decide that your problems have gone on long enough and that you are going to stop them right now and find a way to improve the situation.

Number two is the obvious choice, yet more students each year choose number one — and many caring parents let them choose it. Why would you choose number one?

- You don't know how to fix your problem.

- You have decided you cannot fix your problem.

- You have convinced your school that there is little hope you will make the effort to fix it and so push away the help that could be there for you.

- You have incorrectly convinced yourself that school doesn't matter and that you can get by without giving much thought to it.

Wait! Consider your options.

Look for help. It is not so easy to fill in the holes created by inadequacies in middle school or grade school, but it is much easier to do it now than when you are in mid-life and say, "Oh, did I ever make a mistake." Ask your counselor if there are fundamentals classes to help you. If you get into a class, give it your best and find it isn't much good, keep asking for additional help. It may take time to find the classes that really help you or an alternative school that can fit your needs. Perhaps you can get involved with a computer program that will let you do remedial work at your own speed. Ask about staying after school one or two hours each day to work on a computer self-learning program. Use money from work to hire a tutor. If the first tutor you hire doesn't work for you, find another one. Look for other ideas with your counselor. Don't give up. Keep pushing, asking, struggling, and moving forward until you know enough to do high school work.

Work harder. Maybe you are in the habit of not working very hard. When things are difficult to understand, it is natural to let your attention wander. You will have to change this. You have to say to yourself all the time: "If other people like me can do this, I can figure it out too." And then you have to keep working, in twenty- or thirty-minute blocks of time, until you know the basics that allow you to do high school work.

Improve your English. For many students who come unprepared, the problem is language. If you don't understand enough English to make sense of your classes, you are going to have a hard time. If this is the case for you, turn to Chapter 9 and go to the section on Limited English Proficiency. Also see Chapter 15, Special Education. If there is a big gap between your ability and your achievement, you may qualify for special services.

Relax. High school is designed so that students will graduate. Your school wants you to be there every day, to pass your classes, to walk down the aisle in your cap and gown and receive a diploma with your name on it. Do your part and this will happen.

No doubt you are going to have some screwups in high school — bad days, maybe even bad weeks. Never mind. Put them behind you. Part of what you're learning in high school is how to manage life's highs and lows. The hard times teach us how to deal with disappointment and help us figure out ways to make our lives work. Ride out the lows. Enjoy the successes. Find things that make you laugh. Be kind to others and smile. It will make both you and them feel good. Know that you are changing and growing and that nothing will look quite the same at the end of high school as it does at the start.

Don't be obsessed with college. There are many schools — some of which you may not yet know about — that can offer you a fine post–high school education and a wonderful time. Work diligently in high school, follow the suggestions in this book, and the odds are that you will be able to attend one of them.

Be honest with yourself and with others. Believe in yourself. Look ahead. See problems and deal with them early on. Make up your mind in the ninth grade that you will make high school work for you.

Finding happiness. All of us want to be happy — but happiness is not a pill you buy in the drug store or find under your pillow. Happiness is what comes when we figure out how to work successfully, build satisfying relationships, and intelligently solve the problems that come to us all. Happiness is something you must work toward all of your life, and whether you know it or not, this work has begun. May you do it well and be rewarded with great happiness.

4. The Rules and Requirements

Suppose you meet an incredible athlete who can sink a basketball with one hand, throw a football fifty yards, and jump a high hurdle with ease. But this person comes from some strange and distant place where he never learned any of the rules that govern these sports. Until he learns the rules of the game, he can't play competitively, no matter how much natural talent he brings to his sport. This chapter is about the basic rules that govern high school.

You must understand credits, course requirements, grades, and GPAs to make high school work for you. You must know:

- how many credits you need to graduate
- which courses you are required to take to graduate
- how to calculate your GPA
- what you expect to get from high school in order to plan your courses

Earning Credits

What Is a Credit and What Are Course Requirements? You must have a certain number of points, or **credits**, on your high school record. You get these credits by passing courses. Your schedule is arranged so that you can pass all the courses you need in four years, although some students take longer and some take less time. Usually, each semester of a course equals 1/2 credit. A whole year of a course is one credit, and each credit translates as a "Carnegie unit." Carnegie units are a uniform standard of instructional measurement for schools. One state, Indiana, does not use Carnegie units. In Indiana, a semester course with 250 minutes of instruction per week is officially considered one credit instead of one half credit. A year of Algebra, for example, is two credits. In other words, one Carnegie unit equals two course credits in Indiana.

The courses you take in high school are decided in part by your interests and preferences and in part by the local board of education. In all but three states, a state education board or the legislature sets minimum standards that all students in all districts must meet. Individual districts can raise but not lower those requirements. In Colorado, state requirements are prohibited by law. In Nebraska there are no specific courses required, but high school students must have a minimum of 200 credit hours with 80 percent of these on core curriculum courses. In New Jersey, only a credit of fine arts and half credit of career exploration are mandated as part of the state-required 92 credit hours.

For example, the state of Texas dictates that every high school graduate in Texas have at least 21 credits that include these state requirements:

- 4 years of English
- 3 years of math
- 2 years of science
- 2 years of Social Studies
- 1 semester of U.S. Government and 1 semester of Economics
- 1 1/2 years of Physical education
- 1/2 year of Health
- 7 credits (14 semesters) of electives

The Houston Independent School District (HISD), however, requires all students who begin ninth grade in 1995 or later to have 24 credits to graduate. In addition to the courses listed above, students must add:

- 1 year of foreign language
- 1 year of computer
- 1 more year of Social Studies

- 1 more year of science
- and instead of 7 credits of elective, 3 credits of electives and 3 credits in an area of specialization

HISD students who want an advanced or honors seal on their diplomas will take, in place of the 3 credits of electives:

- 2 more credits of language
- 1 credit of arts

Other cities and states will differ on their requirements for graduation. You want to know exactly what the requirements are in your district by getting a written explanation from your counselor or looking in the school handbook that many high schools distribute to all students.

Course requirements are not there to make a student's life miserable or even difficult. School administrators consult with employers and evaluation experts, teachers and parents to figure out what students need to compete in today's marketplace. The danger is not taking too many demanding or diverse courses; it is taking too few. Some districts, in accord with community values or financial resources, do not require graduates to have all the courses that the most competitive colleges or employers require. Do not assume that because a course is not required, it isn't worth taking.

Below is a suggested minimum core high school program for all students, college-bound or not. This information is based on 1996 Education Commission of the States research using 1992 data. Some states will have undoubtedly upgraded or altered requirements in the intervening years. (See Chapter 13 for a more detailed discussion of why you need core academics.) You will add your own school requirements and electives to this program as your school's schedule permits, and you will adjust it to fit your own needs:

- *4 credits of English* (Already required by all but nine states)

- *3 credits of mathematics* (Required in twenty-six states; other states generally require a minimum of two or two and one half credits, except New York, which requires four math credits)

- *3 credits of history/social studies* (Sixteen states require less than three credits.)

- *3 credits of science* (Only six of the states require three credits. Most require two. Illinois, Minnesota, Montana, and Ohio require only one credit.)

- *2 credits of foreign language* (Only about ten states specify foreign language.)

- *1 credit of Fine Arts* (Only fifteen states specify some fine arts credit, often only one half credit.)

- *1 credit of career- and technology-related classes* (Including computer science. There is a strong national trend to encourage all students, college bound and non-college bound, to have more career- and technology-related classes.)

- *1 credit of physical education/health/sex education* (Most states require one or one and one half credits. A few require two or two and one half. New Jersey stands out with a requirement of 4.5.)

See Chapter 7 for a discussion of what these courses offer and why they are included in the high school curriculum. If a course is not listed above, it doesn't mean you shouldn't take it. For example, I believe many students gain academically and personally from theater classes and if a student takes two years of a foreign language, it makes sense to take a third year and actually learn to speak the language. Yet neither theater nor a third year of language is on the list. There will, of course, be disagreements about just what belongs on this list. Some would urge more than one credit of fine arts; others would say more math, science, or language is important; and still others would insist teens need more career-related courses. My home state of Texas is about to insist every student have at least a half credit of public speaking. I suggest the above course list as a generic baseline for most mainstream students who hope to be competitive in the work place and in college admissions. Make adjustments based on your own circumstances. For example, if you already speak a second language, you may want to substitute more arts and career and technology classes for a language, or you may want to learn a third language or add more math and science.

Pages 28–29 give you a general template for listing your required courses and organizing them year by year. How many courses you can take will depend on how your school divides its school day. Some schools only have room for five or six classes each semester. Others insist on seven or eight. With year-round schools and more decentralized school administration, there is an ever-increasing menu of alternatives.

Copy the following chart so you can use it again and again as you consider different scheduling possibilities.

1. Write in the courses that you are required by your school district under the year you have taken them or plan to take them.

2. Write in the additional courses you have taken or are planning to take. This planner gives you spaces for up to 31 credits. Adjust the layout of the planner to fit your particular circumstances.

3. Put an X on the squares of courses you have already passed.

4. Circle the squares for courses you are taking now but have not yet passed.

5. Now check the courses you have taken and are taking as well as those you plan to take against your district's required courses. You can, if you wish, re-do the chart so it only includes your required courses with all other courses going into the spaces for electives. Make a copy for your counselor. Put a copy on your bulletin board or the refrigerator.

High School Course Planner

Every square (□) represents 1/2 credit, which is usually one semester or one quarter.

	1st Year	2nd Year	3rd Year	4th Year
English:	□ _____	□ _____	□ _____	□ _____
	□ _____	□ _____	□ _____	□ _____
Math:	□ _____	□ _____	□ _____	
	□ _____	□ _____	□ _____	
Social Studies/ History:	□ _____	□ _____	□ _____	
	□ _____	□ _____	□ _____	
Science:	□ _____	□ _____	□ _____	
	□ _____	□ _____	□ _____	
Career and Technology:		□ _____		
		□ _____		

continued on next page

Is Your Counselor Responsible for Making Sure You Meet Your Requirements? In most high schools, you'll have a counselor or an adviser who is responsible for helping you plan your schedule so you meet your requirements and get all the credits you need to graduate. *Do not, however, rely only on your counselor.* He or she may have hundreds of students to watch over, and the truth is that you can get lost in the crush. *You* must be in charge of your school schedule. Talk to counselors, teachers, mentors, parents, and friends to get their ideas and advice and then figure out what is right for you. When it is time to fill in your schedule for the coming semester or coming year, you want to have your own personal plan already sketched out. Whether you meet with your coun-

	1st Year	2nd Year	3rd Year	4th Year
Physical education/ Health:	☐ _____			
	☐ _____	☐ _____		
Additional require- ments and electives:	☐ _____	☐ _____	☐ _____	☐ _____
	☐ _____	☐ _____	☐ _____	☐ _____
	☐ _____	☐ _____	☐ _____	☐ _____
	☐ _____	☐ _____	☐ _____	☐ _____
	☐ _____	☐ _____	☐ _____	☐ _____
Language:	☐ _____		☐ _____	
	☐ _____		☐ _____	
Fine Arts:	☐ _____			
	☐ _____			

Add up all your credits and make sure you have scheduled the number you need to graduate.

selor to pick courses for the coming term in small groups or one-on-one, use this meeting to ask specific questions about your schedule.

Choosing Courses Involve your parents. From the end of eighth grade, every student needs a plan for meeting course requirements, for getting all the necessary credits for graduation, and for leaving high school headed in the direction of success. It is fine to change your plan as ideas and interests develop. What is *not* fine is to be without a plan. Sit down with your parents and look over all the possibilities. Talk about what seems right for you. Your parents may have ideas and suggestions that can get you thinking in a new direction. If you disagree with them, ex-

Checklist for Choosing Courses

In the spring of each year, sit down and review what you have done in school against what you know you must accomplish to graduate. Do this with a parent, an adviser, a mentor, or an adult you respect. Look at the boxes on your planning chart and review what you have taken, what you still plan to take, and whether you want to make changes.

If you have *any* questions, be persistent about getting them answered.

- Don't wait for your counselor to call you.
- Don't assume your counselor will design the best schedule for you.
- Don't check off what the person next to you thinks is good.
- Don't look for the easiest courses.
- Look for what is going to be right for you and where you want to go.

plain and defend your choices. This is a good way to make sure you have chosen well for yourself. If they don't understand the system, teaching them how your high school works is a great way to make sure you understand it yourself. Involving parents in your planning will help you, and then they will have fewer free-floating anxieties about your school life and can support you in your goals instead of nagging you to get some.

If you are running your own show, at any point in your high school career you should know — without having to go to the office and look it up — how many credits you have completed, how many more you need, and in what subject areas.

Unusual Needs Some students have unusual needs or interests, or quite usual ones, that simply don't fit with the school's curriculum or scheduling. It is the rare public school that is prepared to bend the rules or seek waivers from the regulations to accommodate individual needs. You have to understand this from the school's perspective before you can be effective in pressing your own case. Administrators know from experience that if they bend rules and regulations for one student, they open the door to many requests. They may be accused of favoritism or racism in a genuine effort to accommodate one student's situation.

One college-bound student spent his last two years of high school in a magnet school for the performing arts. Because half the day was given to arts-related classes and because the school was relatively small, class choice was limited. This student had gone to summer school after junior year to fit in a senior government and economics requirement but wanted to take both physics and Spanish 4 his senior year — and the only section of each met at the same time. His counselor scheduled him for English, calculus, physics, and library assistant in the four morning academic blocks. His parents suggested they hire a graduate student from the university a few blocks away to tutor him in Spanish during that open period. The principal explained that this would be unsupervised and couldn't be permitted. While the parents were focused on what was best for this child, the principal was focused on another agenda, and one student's ability to read a little more Spanish was not compelling enough to divert her attention. It didn't seem worth a full-scale fight that would probably take longer to play out than the school year so the parents opted to have their son tutored in the evenings. The student switched himself from library assistant to yearbook staff. Said the family, "We never did figure out what the principal's mind-set was. We just knew we were being viewed as troublemakers."

It is quite possible that your school will make decisions that seem unreasonable to you but make good sense to school administrators from their perspectives. Pick your battles carefully. The unpleasant truth is that school administrators can carry out quiet revenge on you because you are annoying. Administrators are going to read this and bristle. I wish it weren't true, but it is. We are all human, and it is natural to be kinder and more helpful to people you like than to people who you think are causing you trouble. It is all too normal to leave the annoying kid with the pushy parents in the overcrowded class or with the most difficult teacher because, after all, somebody has to be there, and this family is already using up its quota of extra attention. This does not mean you should take whatever the school system lays on you or that your school will not listen carefully to your concerns. It does mean that you must understand the consequences for schools when they consider unusual requests, and you must understand the possible consequences for you when you push the system hard.

Getting Answers to Questions — and Having the Courage to Ask the Questions In talking with high school students, I have found that often they know the right question to ask — and they make an effort to get it answered — but when that effort doesn't pay off, they give up. "Counselors never have time for us as students. They are always too busy. Some of them are too rude. They really don't care," a senior high school student wrote in a focus group, echoing the feelings of many of her classmates.

Yes, in a big school bureaucracy, it can be difficult to see your counselor. Counselors have more responsibilities than time. They grow frustrated when students don't do what is asked of them the first time and then come around asking for help. Sometimes they look at a student's record and figure that the student doesn't really care, so they don't make an extra effort for him or her. But most counselors do care. If you establish a personal relationship with your counselors, you are likely to find they are there for you.

This book is meant to make high school easier for both students and parents. But even after reading every page, you are still likely to have questions and confusions. Do *not* give up until you get your questions answered. "I feel stupid asking dumb questions," many teens and even some parents report. No serious question is a dumb question. There is nothing at all stupid about wanting to plan one's life and asking people whose job it is to help you to do just that. In fact, I suggest you stop thinking in terms of dumb and smart and start thinking in terms of understanding or not understanding.

Ask questions! Then, listen to the answer. Try and figure things out. Talk to others. And if you are still confused, *ask again!* Keep pushing for an answer until you get it and understand it. Students are *entitled* to have their questions answered. Many counselors' offices have forms you can fill out to request an appointment. If not, write your own note. Tell the counselor why you want an appointment and include your schedule. Ask the counselor to send for you when he or she has time. If you don't get a response within two days, leave another message.

Alternatively, students or parents can send the counselor a note. Include a return envelope addressed to the student's homeroom or, better yet, a self-addressed, stamped envelope. Ask that you get a written answer in the mail, or ask the counselor to leave the written answer with the office secretary and say when you will pick it up. If your counselor is on e-mail and you are too, this is a great way to communicate.

If you don't get an answer to your question or you don't understand the answer, keep trying. But try to avoid all but the most critical questions the first few weeks of the semester when it is crazy in most every public high school. *Plan ahead!*

There are always a few people who complain that nobody ever explains anything when, in fact, the problem is that they are not listening when the explanations are being delivered. Don't let this be the case with you. The more you seem to be doing for yourself, the more you will inspire others to want to help you.

Attendance

There are five important reasons to attend your classes.

1. Most high schools have clearly established attendance policies. In order to receive credit for a semester class, you may need to limit absences, either the unexcused or the total of all absences. There

may be an appeals process if you go over the number of absences permitted, but the best and easiest solution is just to show up for your classes.

2. You can't learn things you don't hear, see, or touch. If you aren't in class, you're cutting down on your learning possibilities. Analisa Martinez, a high school senior, thinks that her lack of attendance is the number one reason for failing. "I realize now that just missing two days of class can really get you behind, make your grade lower,

---

Attendance

A business co-op teacher in an urban high school discusses the importance of attendance: "The employers we work with . . . look at transcripts of the students we recommend to them. If the student has a poor attendance record, the company figures the person who doesn't come to school regularly isn't going to come to work regularly, and they reject them. So we don't take kids who don't have good attendance into our program because we only have so many spaces, and they go first to students who are most likely to do well in the program."

A welding teacher explains his need to work with students who show up. "Welding class if overcrowded. We can't take all the students who are interested. If a student misses a day, I have to stop and catch him up individually while ignoring the rest of the class. That isn't fair to the students who do show up, so if you can't come to school regularly, you can't be in this class."

The technical coordinator for the Carpenters' International Union reports that when potential apprentices are interviewed, the committee always looks at the transcript, particularly at attendance. "We figure if you didn't show up regularly in high school, we can't count on you on the job. Your attendance record is a big factor in whether you get hired and then to which jobs you are assigned."

---

and have the class discussion become confusing. You *have* to come to class."

3. A poor attendance record in your freshman and sophomore years can keep you out of the career and co-op classes that open the doors to excellent real-world experiences later on. If you learn better by doing than reading and writing, you want to be in those classes. If you skip school, you may wind up being shut out of the very classes you are most likely to want and to enjoy.

4. Employers often use school attendance records as a factor in deciding whom to hire. They want to be sure you will show up for work regularly, and they believe what you have done in school is a good predictor of what you will do on the job.

5. Many schools receive state funds based on student attendance. If you contribute to the absences in your school, you are contributing to a loss of dollars that your school could otherwise use for things that benefit you and your classmates.

If you have a major difficulty and must miss school, make sure you do everything you can to keep up with your work. Here is a helpful tip: at the start of each semester, take a sheet of paper and get the name and home phone of at least two people in each of your classes. Pick people who are organized. Put the paper somewhere safe at home. Then, if you must be absent, call and find out what you missed, what is due the next day, and whether there is going to be a test. You can also call these people if you get confused about an assignment or have a general question.

5. Grades

What Is a Grade Point Average?

Your grade point average (GPA) is a number (the average of all your grades) that reflects your academic performance. Your GPA is the way the world scores school performance; higher scores can bring more opportunity and recognition. GPAs are used in determining athletic and academic scholarships, college admissions, entrance to special programs, and work opportunities. Your GPA allows you to compare your academic performance to that of others in your class.

A GPA is a bit like a batting average in baseball. Every time the batter connects with the ball and gets on base, his or her batting average rises. But in baseball, your batting average doesn't reveal whether you hit a single, a double, or a home run. Your GPA, however, reveals not only whether you hit or strike out in each course but just how well you hit.

If you take a course and fail it, you don't get any credit and it doesn't count toward graduation. That failure may continue to affect your GPA during your entire high school career, even if you take the course over and get a better grade. Some schools will remove a low grade from your average if you repeat the class, but many will not. Like the baseball player's lifetime batting average, your successes and failures follow you. You don't start fresh each year.

How to Calculate a GPA Your GPA is the average of all your class grades. The grade you get for each class has a point value. Generally, the point value follows the convention below. If your school uses a different point system, write it in here:

A = 4.0 points, or 90–100, or _____
B = 3.0 points, or 80–89, or _____
C = 2.0 points, or 75–79, or _____
D = 1.0 points, or 70–74, or _____
F = .9 or below, or below 70, or ____

Some school districts may give point values for minuses and pluses; others bump up the point value for advanced classes. In some school districts, certain high-level classes count an A as 5 points, a B as 4, a C as 3, and a D as 2 to reflect the more demanding nature of these classes (but a 4.0 GPA is still the highest reported average). In the latter situation, you can raise your GPA as well as stretch your brain by taking more difficult classes.

Using the same logic, special education classes in many districts carry a reduced point value, with an A being 3 points, a B being 2, a C 1.5, and a D being 1 point.

Since everybody in a district plays by the same rules, it doesn't matter how your school assigns points. It just matters that you are clear about how the point values work. When applying to college, don't worry about competing against students whose schools may calculate to yield higher GPAs — college admissions people are familiar with the differences in school grading systems and take this, as well as the difficulty of the classes you take, into account when evaluating student applications.

If all your high school classes are worth the same amount of credit (usually, 1/2 credit per semester class in all states except Indiana, where a semester class is one credit), add up the points from each semester grade you have received and divide by the number of classes to get your GPA. (If a semester class is worth one full credit in a system where most classes are worth 1/2, you must double the value of the grade and count the course twice. If the class is worth less, you will have to adjust for that as well by counting the class as less than one.)

Fairness in Grading Just as every batter doesn't face an equally good pitcher — or umpire — every student doesn't get an equally good

How to Calculate a GPA

Suppose your grades at the end of your freshman year are:

English 1A:	B+	English 1B:	A
Algebra 1A:	D	Algebra 1B:	F
U.S. History:	C	U.S. History:	B−
Spanish 1A:	C+	Spanish 1B:	B
Physical education:	B	Physical education:	A
Physical science:	C	Physical science:	B

To figure your GPA:

1. An A is worth 4 points. You have two of them so you have 8 points.
2. You have five B's (disregard the pluses and minuses) and a B is worth 3 points, so you have 15 points.
3. Your three C's are worth 2 points each; this is 6 points.
4. The D is worth 1 point and the F isn't worth anything.
5. Add up all those points, and you have earned yourself 30 grade points in 12 courses. Divide those 30 points by the number of courses, 12, and your GPA is 2.5.

But what if you had worked harder on that algebra class, gotten yourself some after-school help, and spent more time on it instead of giving up? You may have ended up with a C first semester and a C second semester instead of a D and an F. You would have a 3.0 GPA.

continued on next page

teacher. Whether a teacher is good or not, "fair" or not, the student, like the batter, is the one being graded on what happens. Most schools have point systems that aim to make grading as fair as possible, but it is still a subjective process. Worse yet, grading may not accurately measure long-term understanding — which is your ultimate goal. You may have failed to jump through all the homework hoops, dot every "i," and cross

If you look at each semester separately, you ended the first semester with a 2.1 GPA, a C average. Second semester you did well, except for the F in algebra pulling you down, and you had a 2.8. If you had only pulled the F up to a D, you would have had a 3.0, a B average — and the difference between a 2.0 and a 3.0 in academic circles is the difference between hitting a single and a triple in baseball.

When the second semester gets averaged with the first semester, your overall GPA is 2.5. The poor grades are always there, averaging in with your better grades. The fewer poor grades you have, the easier it is to balance them with good grades and earn a GPA that will be an asset to you.

Here is another example from an honors student:

Honors English 1:	B+	Honors English 1B:	A−
Algebra 1A:	B	Algebra 1B:	B
Honors U.S. History:	A−	Honors U.S. History:	B+
Spanish 2A:	A	Spanish 2B:	B
Physical education:	B	Physical education:	A
Biology 1A:	A	Biology 1B:	B

English and history are honors courses, so each grade is bumped up in point value. The two honors A's are worth 5 points each, or 10 points. The two honors B's together are worth 8 points. In the remaining regular classes, this student has three A's, or 3 x 4 for 12 points, and five B's, or 5 x 3 for 15 points. Taking both semesters together, this student has 45 grade points divided by 10 classes, a 4.5, which is higher than an A (although 4.0 may be the highest reported GPA). This happens when you take advanced courses that carry extra credit.

every "t," but you still have a better understanding of the material than a student who gets a high grade and yet five minutes after the class is finished cannot explain what the class was about. But the way the world judges your academic performance is through grades. It is the scoring system at school.

I know that in spite of my very best efforts to treat all students exactly alike when I am grading papers, it doesn't always happen. Terrible handwriting and sloppy presentation can work against you, and perfectly typed material can give you an edge. My own fatigue affects how carefully I read a paper and the grade that I give it. The first paper to be graded may get treated more stringently or more generously than the last papers. Even teachers who read through all the papers once and then go back for a second reading may have trouble deciding whether something is a B− or C+, a B+ or an A−, and so on.

Here are some of the subjective factors that subtly influence grading:

Preconceived notions. If your name is on the paper, your teacher is likely to have some ideas about the kind of work you do before he or she begins grading. Teachers expect "good" work from good students and so are primed to look for quality. If you are perceived as a poor student, you can work against the perception by talking with the teacher before you hand in your paper. Explain that you have decided to break the cycle, and you are trying for an A or B on your paper. Ask for help or a review of a draft in advance. This only works, however, if you then submit better work than that which got you your less-than-wonderful academic reputation.

Presentation. Neatness matters. The way your work looks is taken as an indication of how much pride you have in what you have done. Typed work looks better than handwritten work. If you don't have access to a computer, see about getting a typewriter. Second-hand typewriters can be found inexpensively. If you must handwrite, make an extra effort to do so neatly. Use only black or blue ink, not other colors. Don't hand in smudged or scratched-over work if you want to create a positive impression. You don't need fancy folders or laser-designed covers. A simple, well-organized cover page can send the same positive message.

Following instructions. Suppose your history teacher has a rule that every page has your name, your grade, and your homeroom in the upper left hand corner starting on the second line of the page and continuing not more than four inches across the page. Ignore the rule, and you start this teacher off in the frame of mind to deduct points before he or she ever gets to the important stuff. You may consider these annoying details irrelevant, but your ability to listen, remember, and follow instructions will be extremely relevant in the work world — and it's silly to spoil your grade because you didn't pay attention to a simple instruction like where to put your name.

Timeliness. If you are given more days than other students to work on your paper or project, then you have an extra advantage. And because of this, many teachers penalize students who don't hand in their work on time. Don't devalue good work by doing it late. If you have a difficult situation that makes it hard to meet your due date, talk with your teacher before the deadline.

Attitude. Students who display a bad attitude in class or in conversation are inviting closer scrutiny — and tougher grading. Teachers are human, and they are likely to respond in ways similar to the rest of us. If students can't resist the opportunity to knock a smug classmate down a peg or two, don't expect teachers to always resist either.

Honesty. Never cheat. Once a person gets a reputation for copying other people's work or copying from books without citing the author, even original work will be suspect. If you develop a reputation for dishonesty, it is incredibly difficult to shake — and you are judged more closely and more harshly.

If it's fair to say that all grading is not completely objective, it's foolish to argue that because of this, grades are unimportant. A single grade can be off-base, but the sum of all your grades is usually a fair reflection of the quality of work you are doing.

Your GPA, the average of all your grades, will be a key factor in your being considered for most academic and athletic scholarships, admission to special programs, selection for honors and awards, and admission to competitive colleges. GPAs often play a part in determining who is recommended for employment and who is hired for jobs. Sometimes grades are used as a cutoff, a designated limit. For example, anyone with a 3.0

or better gets considered for an interview; anyone below a 3 is simply not considered, even though the difference between a 3.0 and a 2.9 in real life is not significant when comparing real people. Is this fair? Maybe not, but it's convenient when there's no easy way to evaluate lots of people in a limited amount of time, and it happens often.

Grades are a code used by the world outside high school. Good grades suggest that you are likely to be reliable, responsible, and intelligent. Bad grades make people worry about your ability to follow through, understand what is required, and do what is expected. Many intelligent people get bad grades — but when they do so consistently, they are not being intelligent about how the real world works or about managing their own high school careers.

Now that I have emphasized just how important grades are, I want to add a warning: it is possible to put too much emphasis on grades. Maybe only A's are acceptable to you or your parents. High standards are very desirable, and if they are leading you to success and positive self-esteem, don't change a thing. But if insistence on uniformly high performance is causing family conflict, stress expressed in physical symptoms, or unpleasant self-doubt, then the cost may be too high. Everyone is different. Wise parents must pay lots of attention to those differences, and you'll help your parents by talking to them about how their expectations make you feel.

If your parents are complaining about your grades and you know you're not making much of an effort, the best thing is to own up to the truth. Admit you're not working hard and then start talking with them about why it seems difficult to be more disciplined. Sometimes what students consider to be working "hard" is not that hard. But if you feel you're giving a tremendous effort, you must be clear about that as well. Effort is, in the long run, more important than grades. For example, a gifted student who is sliding by and learning little may get an A but deserves no praise. Someone who must struggle more but puts heart and soul into a course and ends up with a B− is, in the end, the wiser and richer student and deserves the praise of parents and teachers.

Here are a few points to keep in mind when thinking about grades:

Grades are important, but they're not as important as learning. The worst part about bad grades is that they usually mean a student invested a lot of time attending class for very little return. What we know and how well we have taught ourselves to learn difficult material and hold on to it will be with us long after a single high school grade has any importance. Spend a semester in class to get a D or an F and a chunk of life that will never come around again may have been wasted. Spend time mastering something difficult and (whether you earn an A or a C) that knowledge is yours forever. If a difficult course is required to gain entry to a program that interests you, bite the bullet, put in the time, and conquer it. Grades count, but what you learn counts for more and for a longer time.

Don't assume that because another student is working faster, she necessarily has taken hold of the material. If you have to give up some grade points to spend additional time actually "owning" the material, do it.

If you get straight A's in high school but you aren't involved in any extracurricular activity, such as sports, theater, the community, a job, volunteer work, or special hobbies, you will be missing out on part of your education. College admissions people look for well-rounded students. Strive for a balance in your life. Learning comes in many ways, and you cannot be sure where you'll find just what you need.

Grades are not a measure of your worth as a person. A class grade indicates how well you mastered the material in that class and followed the requirements of the teacher. Academically gifted students who don't bother with assignments can get bad grades; students with little intellectual curiosity or imagination who are diligent can earn outstanding grades. Grades don't measure your personal worth, but they do report on your ability to absorb information in the school environment and fulfill requirements in a particular situation.

Jeremy was a good math student who enrolled in calculus in eleventh grade and finished the first semester with a D. Jeremy did not admire his teacher — and the teacher did not admire Jeremy, especially since he seldom completed his homework. He dropped the class at the end of the semester, and then signed up again senior year with a different teacher to repeat first semester and go on to second semester. Jeremy loved his teacher that year, earned an A for both semesters, and was nominated for a math award. He did not become a more adept math student between junior and senior year. With a different teacher, he had a different attitude. His new teacher inspired and challenged him, and he responded well.

In this story, is the first teacher a "bad guy" and the second teacher a "good guy"? One teacher will do very well with some kinds of students but not so well with others. Some of the students in Jeremy's eleventh grade calculus class earned A's and managed to do well. Jeremy, however, decided he would punish what he regarded as bad teaching with bad performance.

One of the most important lessons of high school is that life is not fair. It wasn't "fair" for Jeremy to have a teacher who so uninspired him when he was, as events proved, so capable of being inspired. But we all meet bosses, colleagues, and customers who don't inspire us or make it easy for us to do what we have to do. The exceptional people are those who figure out how to cope in difficult situations, how to turn problematic situations around, and make those situations work. Jeremy paid a high price in terms of time and grade penalty for his solution. He would have learned valuable people skills as well as calculus if he'd committed himself to working with his first teacher instead of making a statement about his dissatisfaction, which had no effect except to hurt his GPA. If, however, you really clash with a teacher or cannot learn with a particular person, withdraw from the class instead of failing it.

Distinguish between working for grades and working for yourself. The reason to get good grades is not to please the teacher but to open doors to the greatest number of opportunities. You might not care about geometry class and have trouble believing it will have much influence in your later life, but you might care a great deal about, say, flying airplanes — and it turns out that a competitive program to give students solo flying lessons uses grades to choose who can apply. Better grades equal greater opportunities.

Often, you don't start figuring out what direction you want to go after high school until junior or senior year. However, the grades you earned in ninth and tenth grade, when you didn't have a clue about what you might want, are still being averaged into your GPA. If friends want to know why you are working so hard on schoolwork now, tell them, "When I learn enough to know what I want to do with my life, I don't want any old business getting in my way."

Good work takes time. Typically there is a relationship between how much time one spends on schoolwork and the grade given to the work. Teens who will spend hours practicing free shots at the hoop over the garage or in the playground in order to get good at scoring expect to learn Spanish verbs, chemistry formulas, or grammar rules in five minutes. Teens who would never tell a boss, "I don't need to spend an hour stocking these shelves so neatly. I can do it really fast in fifteen minutes, and it will be almost as good and I can be out of here," tell themselves it's O.K. to rush through schoolwork and move on to something else.

Sometimes it makes sense to settle for a lower grade. The standard do-well message is: Get A's. If you can't get an A, get a B, but do the very best you can. Sometimes, however, teens need to be told, "Get a B . . . or get a C." Of course, this has to do with trade offs. If you are completely absorbed by and delighted with a particular aspect of learning — it might be a science fair project or a musical performance, a term paper that has mushroomed into a passion or a fascination with butterflies — you may find there is simply not enough time to do everything well. Academic passions are a gift and a joy, and they should be honored and well cared for whenever they arise. In some instances, it may be worth doing less well in one area to excel in others.

You may avoid taking a harder class because you don't want to risk getting less than an A. What you risk instead is learning less, stretching less, being less. Remember that this education is for you, not the college admissions officer. Take the courses that are good for *you*. Don't be afraid of experimenting with a course in mechanics because you think it isn't academic enough. And don't be afraid of taking a college-prep course in creative writing or advanced biology if you feel the urge just because you told your counselor or your friends you are not on the college track.

What You Need to Know About Semester Grades

Most schools spell out what is required to pass a class. Often, there is a formula for how the final grade is to be computed. For example, in a semester class with three grading periods, a school district might determine that the final grade will be made up of the average of your final grade for each of three six-week grading periods and the grade on the course final. These six-week grades, a teacher might explain, will be determined by giving 20 percent weight to classroom participation, 40 percent weight to homework assignments, 20 percent to the term paper, and 20 percent to the mid-term exam given each grading period.

You should know if there is a guiding formula for your classes and what it is. So ask! For example, using the formula above, a student who is diligent about completing all homework on time and participating intelligently in class discussions can influence 60 percent of his or her grade without the stress of testing. Another 20 percent can be easily controlled by giving serious effort to one's term paper. If you nail down B's for all of these, you can fail the mid-term exam and still get a C+ for the grading period. On the other hand, you can pass each grading period and fool yourself into thinking you'll have no problems passing each course.

Watch how easy it is to shoot yourself in the foot if you are not careful: in many school districts, students need to accumulate 280 points per class to pass, and teachers give number, not letter, grades. Suppose you are just squeaking through, not really paying attention and, from time to time, copying the homework from a friend. You get a 72 the first six weeks, a 74 the second six weeks, and only a 70 the last six weeks — not very good, but, you say to yourself, a 70 is a D and still passing. However, come the final, you don't know much because you haven't really been learning the material, and you score a 60. In spite of having passing grades for each six-week period, you fail the course for the semester because when those three D's valued at 72, 74, and 70 are combined with a failing grade of 60 on the final, they add up to only 276 points or an F.

In many school districts, the lowest grade you can earn on your report card in one of the semester's reporting period is a 50. That means that if you completely botch it for one six-week period, you are not so far in the hole that it becomes impossible to earn enough points in other grading periods to pass the class. But on a final exam, you can go below a 50. You can, if you don't show up, get a zero; there is no grade barrier here to protect you. Doing badly on a final exam doesn't doom you to failure, however, if you have kept all your other grades high.

Know What Is on Your Transcript A transcript is a single sheet of paper that summarizes your entire school record. Colleges use your transcript to review your academic career. Employers may use it to get a sense of what kind of employee you will be. The National College Athletic Association uses it to determine recruitment eligibility. Your transcript reports your classes, your grades, your attendance, and your conduct. It will also have your standardized test scores on it.

Like any other piece of paper in this world, it can have mistakes. If the person who caused the mistake has long left the high school or doesn't remember your discussion about changing a grade, you can be in a bad place. Avoid this by reviewing your transcript regularly. Ask your counselor for a copy or go directly to the school registrar. Some schools will ask you to fill out a form and, perhaps, pay $1.00 for a copy. This is well worth a dollar. If you are already a junior or senior and have never seen your transcript, get a copy immediately.

Here is why: sometimes students recall that they took a course and they did not. Sometimes they assume a teacher has changed a grade as agreed but the change is not on the transcript. Sometimes they remember that they passed a class but it is not reflected that way on the transcript. If you never check, you may arrive at the end of senior year and be unpleasantly surprised to find that the transcript does not report what you thought it would.

6. How Do You Choose Courses?

Imagine that you pack up the car, eager to start a family vacation — but as you pull out of the driveway, you still aren't sure whether to go to the New England seashore, the Houston Space Center, or Disneyland. How do you know which way to turn when you get to the highway? And once you pick your direction, you'll need to decide the route: are you gunning for the best time; do you want the most scenic route; is it important to stop for lunch with Aunt Julia?

The point is, if you don't know what you want out of high school or where you are headed, it's difficult to choose your courses. Now, some of you will argue, "What difference does it make? I'll take what they tell me and figure out where I am going when the time is right." Years and years ago, you might have gotten by with that strategy. But the world is tougher now and drifting through high school today puts you in danger of marching nowhere with your life. Why let someone else decide your interests when you can and should decide for yourself?

The courses you take in high school make a *big* impact on the directions in which you're likely to head after high school. High school provides terrific opportunities to sample ideas and experiences. The more ideas and experiences you sample, the more you come to understand about yourself and the world and the more information you have to help you make decisions. You don't need to graduate from high school with answers, but it helps if you can use high school to shape specific questions, questions like: Do I need college to pursue my interest in marine life? Is the arts the area in which I want to focus my work life? Since working with my hands makes me happy, how can I use this information in developing a career plan?

Because it is so incredibly difficult for most of us to figure out what we want to do when we grow up, there is a powerful urge to avoid the question. Adults often feel overwhelmed by the question, so don't be surprised if you do, too. You don't need to come up with a final answer in high school. But you should be thinking this and trying on ideas for size. Don't do what others are doing simply because it's the easy way out. It is the lucky people who find a passion early or who have people in their lives who guide, nudge, urge — and sometimes just plain push — them to see a variety of possibilities and to prepare for a range of opportunities. If you are a person whose parents are pushing you to explore a career possibility and you are resisting without any alternative ideas, stop for a minute and ask yourself: What is the worst that could happen if I do such and such — and what is the best? If the worst is nothing much and the best seems pretty good, why not give it a try? Or come up with your own alternative plan.

If you are interested in applying to the most competitive colleges, your courses must be planned carefully. In smaller school districts, it may be difficult to fit in all the courses that you want — and need — to take because courses are not offered every semester or the few sections fill up quickly. In larger districts, you may have too many choices. In both large and small school districts, many schools are overcrowded and can't accommodate all requests. This is one reason for tentatively planning out all four years as a freshman. It may take careful planning to figure out how to meet the competitive admission requirements of colleges or specialized training programs while also addressing your own requirements.

If you think college is not for you, your high school courses will be even more important because your options are less clearly defined. You also want to give yourself room to change your mind about college later. See Chapter 12, Using School to Start Your Career.

The following points will help you choose your courses intelligently.

Know Your Goal Pick a destination — a college, a career path, a consuming interest or a specific goal (graduating with honors, for example), the military, or becoming certified in a technical skill. But don't stop there! Find out exactly what you need to get to that place — don't guess. Once you know what path will lead you toward your goal, then start, one step at a time, moving along it. *You* are the driver on this journey. Decide where to go. You can change goals along the way, but don't drift, waiting for a goal to suddenly appear. Understand that college and career goals can be pursued at the same time.

Weigh Easy vs. Hard Some students choose the easiest classes so they can get A's and B's without much work. If you were in training for a marathon, you wouldn't choose the easiest, slowest workout every

Honors Classes

Cindy was an honor student in middle school. She was offered the chance to take pre-IB (International Baccalaureate, which is an honors program) classes in ninth grade but decided to stick with her friends in regular classes. She found her classes easy but boring. She wasn't very interested, and her grades were mostly B's.

A mentor convinced her to sign up for some IB classes in tenth grade. Cindy worried that these classes would be too hard. The classes were, in fact, more demanding — but they were more interesting. They moved faster and she didn't daydream. Cindy had to work harder but knew she was learning more and improving her academic skills. She earned a B, and it pushed her average up because the IB class was worth more points, and Cindy felt good about herself and what she learned.

Joachim's experience was just the opposite. He was placed in several honors classes and found the pace so fast that he didn't have the time to learn the material the way he needed to. He shifted some of his subjects to regular classes. By moving at a slightly slower pace he felt he was learning more, and he was able to get mostly A's, which helped him when he applied for college scholarship assistance.

day. Since you are in training for the rest of your life, don't choose classes that won't prepare you to run a good race. If you are in doubt, choose the more difficult class. If you find the class too difficult, you can move to an easier one. Grades are important, but developing academic skills is more important. No matter how hard a course, you must take it and master it if it is required for your success. For example, many students struggle with higher level math, but need it for college or career training. You *can* do it if you don't panic, work hard, and stay positive and focused.

Fight for What You Need Sometimes you may be placed in a class you didn't request because there is space and it fits your schedule. If this is not the right class for you, insist that you be changed — and quickly, because these switches often must occur in the first seven to ten days of the semester. To change classes, be persistent. Go early to your counselor's office; stay late; write your counselor a note explaining the need for a class change (and keep a copy for yourself), or ask a parent or mentor to help you.

My children started school in a small public school system that made students and parents feel very welcome. Then they attended private schools. Because private schools charge tuition, they have an added incentive to be responsive to parents and students; if these "customers" are not satisfied, they will go elsewhere. When we moved to Houston, our sons re-entered public school. One morning, I was coaching our ninth grader on how to handle a school problem he was having. Our older son interrupted me: "Mom, you don't understand. We aren't in private school anymore. You can't tell him how to handle this himself. In public school, they don't listen to kids. You have to go over there and fight for him."

I tell you this story not to put down public schools. There are many public schools that do listen to students and that are highly responsive to the needs of students and parents. But in many overcrowded and financially strapped districts, the demands are great, the resources are limited, and the staff is frequently harried. There are times when an adult can be more effective than a student. If you feel that your school isn't listening to you, ask a parent or another adult to guide you in being heard.

Get Planning Help It is a common practice to have students fill out a choice sheet each spring with their class selections for the coming year. The student signs it; in some schools a parent or guardian is also required to sign. Usually, counselors meet with students in groups or individually to explain course choices.

If you have questions, this book can help, but don't stop here. Talk to others. Ask teachers you admire what classes they suggest you take. Ask juniors, seniors, or recent graduates who seem to be on track for their advice. Talk with mentors, employers, and advisers. Definitely speak to your parents and encourage them to talk with other parents whose kids are ahead of you in school. Of course, if you do all this talking, you will get conflicting advice. Don't worry; that's normal. What you want are lots of ideas to take home, spread out on the kitchen table, and consider. You can do this on your own, but if you have parents who can support you in the process, take advantage of your good fortune and let them get involved. As you select courses, go over the planning chart on pages 28–29 and review your original plan to see if it still seems right for you.

Think Ahead If new ideas about course selection come into focus for you during the summer, call your counselor before school starts in the fall. If possible, arrange an appointment with the counselor before school starts or, if this can't happen, leave a note (keep a copy) with a stamped, addressed envelope and your phone number so the counselor can respond easily. Most high school counselors will be back at least two weeks before school starts. Do yourself and your counselor a big favor and deal with necessary changes before the fall semester begins. Making changes during the first week of school is a major pain for everybody.

Do it if you must, but try to avoid getting into this situation by thinking ahead.

Other Ways to Meet Your Requirements

If you are unable to meet your course requirements during the school day, there are two other ways of satisfying course requirements:

Correspondence Courses Most states have approved high school correspondence courses. Usually they are offered in conjunction with selected state universities. In Mississippi, for example, Mississippi State and Southern Mississippi are the two schools through which high school students can receive high school credit for correspondence courses. Most, but not all, states limit how many credits you can earn this way. In Mississippi, students can take two courses. High school seniors, however, can take four courses. Mississippi students have one year in which to complete the material (with two three-month extensions available at $5 per extension) and can retake the final exam once for $10. The cost as we go to press is $55 for one half-unit course plus book costs, but pricing is currently under review. In 1995–96, about 3,100 high school students completed high school correspondence courses for credit at Mississippi State. About five hundred additional students registered but failed to complete classes in the required time.

While the details will vary from state to state, you can expect a similar structure around the country. You'll have to get your high school counselor or principal's permission to receive credit for a correspondence course; you must contact the recognized university extension programs; you'll have a fixed time in which to complete the course work and take the exam; you will be able to retake the exam one time.

Credit-by-Exam You may be able to earn high school credit by passing district or state credit-by-exam tests. Usually, the requirements for being allowed to do this are strict. You may need to have a certain GPA. You will need to score at a certain level and may need your counselor's permission. If you are ready for a higher level course but cannot take it without credit in lower level courses, this may be a good strategy for you. If you want to graduate early, bypass course work in subjects you feel you already know or develop a knowledge base in something that is not taught at your school, you might choose credit-by-exam.

In some parts of the country, you can take a course test, get the results and decide whether to ask for credit-by-exam or to cancel the results. Some districts offer these exams at no charge and others have a fee. Do not be surprised if your counselor is unfamiliar with the rules and regulations for credit-by-exam. This is not an option many students exercise. For more information, call your school board and ask to speak to the person who oversees independent credits.

Night School and Dual Credit Classes If you are organized and energetic, you can take a course in night school at the same time that you are attending day school. Check with your high school district about night school offerings. Another possibility in some districts is dual credit with local colleges. You can take a college course for credit and have it count toward a high school requirement as well. You can take the course in the late afternoon or evening; in some circumstances, you can take it during your school day.

The Pace of Your Schedule — Speeding Up or Slowing Down

Today there are greater variations in school schedules. Maybe your high school day has six, seven, or eight periods. Maybe your district has two semesters with three six-week grading periods. Maybe it has quarters, blocks, alternating days, or year-round schooling. Whatever the current configuration in your high school, high school programs are designed so you can graduate in four years.

Although most students can comfortably finish high school in four years, you may decide to finish in less or more time. You can usually continue in high school until the school year in which you turn 21. If you must work and don't have enough energy for school, slow down, take fewer classes, and learn more. It may be better to graduate a bit later, having studied hard, taken advantage of the academic and career courses offered and gotten good grades, than to push through in four years without learning all that you could.

If you are a strong student aiming for college, you might slow down enough to take more Advanced Placement (AP) classes than you could handle normally and study very hard so that you can take the AP exams (for which there is a fee) and pass with high grades. Or you may take college classes through your high school. In this way, you may accumulate enough credits to enter college with advanced status and save a semester or two of college tuition. (Check out the regulations for slowing down or speeding up with your particular district. There will be different rules in different schools. Call your school board and ask to speak to the person in charge of attendance policies.)

Remember, you won't graduate if you don't meet all your requirements, so make sure you know what they are and how you are going to meet each one. But more important than the school district's requirements are *your* requirements. Decide what you want from high school; then set out to get it. Learn what you need to know to accomplish your personal goals. If your school can't provide you with everything you need, look for summer courses, private tutorials, or work experiences. Teenagers who are wise enough to use their four years of high school to prepare for life after high school are way ahead of the crowd.

7. Subject by Subject

Why Must I Take This Class?

Yes, some classes are boring or difficult. And yes, some of the things you learn in school will slide off you like soap in the shower. But what you *don't* know can hurt you down the line. Here is the most important truth: if you figure out how to learn material whether you like it or not, if you meet the challenge of learning subjects you find difficult or boring and develop the discipline and concentration to get through high school successfully, you learn *much* more than the required English, math, and science. You will learn how to think and solve problems and make plans. You will be able to focus, be organized, follow directions and complete assignments on time. You will express yourself in a way that others can follow. You will be able to figure out how different events or ideas are connected. It will be no problem to deal with numbers sufficiently to make good decisions at home and at work.

These skills are the ones that will be in demand in the workplace in your lifetime. You may slide through high school without them, but you are not likely to slide successfully through the twenty-first century without them. People with these skills stand a good chance of doing well in life. People who don't figure out how to get these skills are more likely to struggle both financially and emotionally. *This is why your classes matter!*

Math was my own black hole. Although I managed to get to calculus, it was a struggle all the way. I vividly remember sitting in geometry class thinking, "Why in the world am I here? I will never need these proofs; I will never remember them. I don't have a clue what they really mean. This is a waste of my time." It never occurred to me as a sophomore in high school to ask, "Just why is it that we are required to take this; why does the world in general think this is important for me to learn, and how can I find the beauty in this subject that people who love it do?"

There is beauty and excitement in every field of study. There is something of value for each of us in every class. And while a talented teacher can make your subjects come alive for you, not all teachers are able to work this magic. I know that I have difficulty learning something if I don't have any idea why I am learning it or how I might use it. Perhaps the same is true for you. This chapter aims to help you understand what each subject area has to offer you.

English. Words have started wars and caused people to fall in love. They have influenced the behavior of millions and changed the course of human events. Words are powerful, and English classes are about letting you share in that power.

English class is all about words — about how you use them, say them, write them, understand them. Grammar, syntax, themes, book reports, oral presentations, bibliographies — these are tools to train you to be an effective word warrior. The fewer words you know, the less you can explain, describe, and express. The more words you know, the more you can articulate, explicate, or delineate, and, according to research, the more likely you are to be successful in your life.

Before people really get to know you, they form some fast opinions about you. These opinions are especially influenced by your physical appearance and by the way you communicate — your spoken, written, and body language. Lessons taught in English class can help you create a favorable impression and be an effective communicator. Suppose you know there is a better way to do something at work and want to convince the boss, or you want to explain to a boyfriend or girlfriend exactly how you feel, or you'd like to get your coworkers to listen to and respect your ideas. You may have great ideas or an excellent understanding of people and situations, but if you cannot put into spoken and written words what you are thinking so that other people can "get it," what you think won't count. It will help you if you can effectively convey your thoughts into spoken and written words. Sometimes people fight or get themselves in difficulty only because they are unable to find the words to explain themselves.

Your English classes will help you:

- learn and use correct grammar so people listen to your message, not your mistakes

- build vocabulary so you can express yourself clearly and precisely — so you know how to say what you think and feel

- write clearly so you can use written expression to convince others of your ideas or opinions, give employers a good accounting of your work and explain your feelings to people you care about

- become comfortable speaking so you can gain the attention and confidence of others

Reading books, poems, and stories are ways to understand how other people feel and think. Literature deepens our understanding of human emotions and behavior. Writing about what we have read teaches us to organize our thoughts and feelings and express them to others. Learn these skills in your English classes and you are preparing well for your future. Without them, you have a handicap in life.

If English is not your native language, you have an advantage and a disadvantage. The advantage is that you will be bilingual — a very important factor in the twenty-first century. The disadvantage is that you may have to work harder in your English classes. But the better you speak and write English, the better you can take advantage of your bilingual capabilities. Don't hold back if you don't know words or make mistakes in grammar. Make mistakes and encourage friends to correct you. Jump in; decide you will get all you can from every English course.

Why Is Reading Extremely Important for Everybody?

Of all the academic skills that you learn in school, reading is the most important. Know how to read well and you can teach yourself anything, go anywhere, walk in anyone's shoes.

With books in your life, you never have to be bored, and you never have to be ignorant about something that interests you. With a book, you can be confined to your bed and still explore the world. With a book, you get your own private tutor right beside you to teach you how to clean a carburetor, cook a gourmet Chinese meal, put on eye makeup like a movie star, or anything else you wish to learn.

If in middle school or high school you are finding that reading is still difficult, *get help.* There is no more important thing you and your parents can do than get you help if you are reading poorly. Give up cars, clothes, trips — whatever you can — to get the help that improves your ability to read and your enjoyment of reading. If you read with difficulty, you won't want to read. The less you read, the less likely you will improve yourself.

Classes to Choose. You should take four years of English classes. Frequently these focus, in successive years, on grammar and writing, American literature, British literature, and world literature. Students who still need to improve their English language skills may substitute English as a Second Language for some English classes. Courses like journalism, practical writing skills, or creative writing are usually elective credits, although in some schools they count toward the required English credits.

Mathematics. More high school students seem to have trouble with math than any other subject, including students who can compute batting averages in their heads or figure out to the inch how much material a sewing pattern requires.

Some of us handle numbers with ease; others struggle. But for all of us, math is becoming more interwoven into everyday life. Today, more companies want their employees to be "math literate." Almost every community college requires degree students to pass a college algebra class. That means any career that requires a community college associate degree may be closed to you if you can't pass the math class.

Do you like working on cars? You are going to need math to work on their electronic systems. Want to work your way up in the building trades? You can't enter some apprenticeship programs without competency in algebra. Think you would be a good restaurant manager? How will you calculate the pounds of potatoes and gallons of milk to order, how will you project your monthly net revenue as a percentage of your total costs?

Suppose you are going out to dinner. You will need to figure how much tip to leave as a percentage of the total bill. Buying clothes? Don't you want to know whether the expensive suit that is on sale for 25 percent off is more or less than the one you don't like as much that isn't on sale? Which interest rate is a better deal for you, the one that is 7.5 percent for ten years with a fee of 2 percent of the loan or the one that is 8.2 percent with no fee? How will you compare the exact financial advantages of a three-year car loan versus a five-year car loan? Our everyday lives are filled with mathematics, and if you don't grasp the basics, you can easily be deceived by others or even by yourself.

Don't let a fear of math stand in the way of doing what you want with your life. You don't have to be good in math to get through algebra and geometry. If you put in the time, you can get hold of it. Math is very logical. It follows specific rules. Those rules can seem confusing unless you come to understand that, in fact, they are a short-hand way of organizing the world of numbers. For example, if you are told to add 1/4 and 3/6, you must convert both fractions to a common denominator. If you pick up four apples and six bananas and I ask how much you have, you are likely to tell me that you have ten pieces of fruit. In doing that, you have converted apples and bananas into a common denominator of fruit in order to add them together — without even thinking about the math rule of choosing a common denominator. Look for ways to understand what the math rules mean, and it will be easier to hold on to them.

If you have access to a computer, there are many programs that can help you learn and give you drills to make sure you understand math. There are also many self-help study books that you can use to supplement your teacher's explanations. You may want to write stories or essays about mathematical ideas as a way to get your hands around the concepts before you start to solve problems. In math classes, you should be looking for the *aha!* — that feeling that comes when suddenly the pieces to a puzzle fall into place and you understand something new that you didn't see before. If you get the right answers but aren't sure how you got them, you're not ready to move on to the next concept. This is because there is a good chance that when you next need to solve a similar problem, you may find yourself unsure how to handle it.

Classes to Choose. Everybody takes Algebra I. The basic mathematics sequence is to take Algebra I in ninth grade, unless you already completed this in eighth grade, followed by geometry, followed by Algebra II. Students who are able should continue with a fourth year of math, especially students interested in science and technology.

If you have great difficulty with math, you may be able to take an expanded algebra course that moves at a slower rate and has lots of math review. It is not a course designed to meet the needs of college or technology-oriented employers. Don't take expanded algebra because you think it will be easier. However, if by taking the slower course you can master the concepts, you can then move on to Algebra II and be competitive for college and higher-level jobs. Some schools also offer a nontraditional algebra sequence for students who need even more intensive instruction. Once you have completed Algebra I, your school may permit you to take math classes that focus on using math in everyday life situations rather than symbolic math. These classes can be helpful, but they don't prepare you for college or for many career training programs. Take as much symbolic math as you possibly can.

Other math courses that give you good preparation for further education and career opportunities include: Precalculus, Trigonometry with either Elementary Analysis or Analytic Geometry, Computer Mathematics, Probability and Statistics, and Calculus. Advanced students may have a chance to take classes or do independent study in Number Theory, Linear Algebra, Linear Programming, History of Mathematics, or Survey of Mathematics.

Mathematically Gifted. Some schools offer independent study programs for very talented math students who need to move ahead faster than most high school students. If you are ready to move at an accelerated pace, ask the head of the math department about the high school math programs at universities, (Duke and Stanford, for example, have such programs) that allow gifted young mathematicians to advance using computer instruction or about taking classes at local colleges. Many universities have programs that permit high school students to earn both college and high school credits for courses.

Science. To consider yourself an educated person, you need an understanding of the world around you. The discipline of science gives you the tools to describe, discuss, and manipulate that world. With a knowledge of science we better understand the air we breathe, the lights in our room, the cars we drive, and our own bodies.

If you play video games on the computer, have dental work performed without feeling the pain, receive immunizations, happily snack on lowfat cookies, or pick up messages from a beeper and return them on a portable phone, you are engaging in the application of scientific principles.

Understanding science allows us to go beyond what our experience tells us to a more revealing way of knowing and understanding. For example, it is easy to believe the world is flat based on what we see. But believing the world is flat because it seems, intuitively, to make sense, prevents us from understanding what is truly happening in the universe. Facts are the basic ingredients for creativity. Without having a base of fact, you are unlikely to be able to invent a new and interesting pattern or possibility.

Every time you bump up against something in a science class that makes you think, "This just doesn't make any sense," you are perfectly positioned to learn something. If you will *welcome* that confusion, stick with it and work through it instead of backing away from it, you will become an educated person.

The study of science does not mean we exclude using feelings and intuition or religious ideals. Feeling is undeniably important to all of us. One reason students are encouraged to study the arts is to develop their feelings. But as we must not ignore feeling, we must not ignore scientific data. Science requires specific vocabularies, mastery of fundamental concepts that shape each discipline, and an understanding of the accepted rules in the various scientific disciplines. Science and technology are growth areas. Those who refuse to develop their scientific understanding deny themselves huge pieces of the twenty-first-century culture — and many employment opportunities.

Science is difficult for many students because it introduces words and concepts that are confusing. Don't decide you can't understand a science class when, in fact, the problem may be that you don't know the words that explain the ideas. Remember, the applications are familiar to you. Think of your study of science as a great puzzle in which each piece of learning is a critical piece.

Classes to Choose. Usually, in ninth grade, students choose physical sciences followed by Biology I and Chemistry I or they take Biology I, Chemistry I, and then Biology II, Chemistry II, or Physics I. The most traditional academic sequence is Biology,

Chemistry, Physics (with Physical science in the eighth grade if possible). In many districts, only courses in these subject areas may count toward meeting the science requirements for advanced diplomas. If you want the most competitive preparation, you should take advanced courses and then take a fourth year of a level II science class in biology, chemistry, or physics — unless you have a special interest in something like astronomy.

For students who find sciences especially difficult, some schools offer survey courses which may be taken in place of Physical science and/or Biology I. A recent trend is toward field-based classes that take students, for example, to rivers or forests to connect the theory to the real world.

Other likely science courses may include Physics II, Geology, Meteorology, Astronomy, Marine science, Environmental science, Laboratory Management, Physiology, and Anatomy. Good science classes have a laboratory component to them.

History/Social Studies. Although it isn't always clear sitting in history class, history is great gossip. History is about who did what to whom, when, why, where, and how. It reveals the family secrets of countries and nations. Social Studies is the extended family of history in which we find anthropology, archaeology, economics, geography, law, philosophy, political science, psychology, religion, and sociology. Each offers a different slant on how to interpret past and present events.

Knowing about the past helps enormously in understanding the present. Think of your own family. Doesn't it help to understand where people came from, what they did, and how they met in order to understand your family today? The same is true for nations.

Look at just a few examples: think about race relations in America today. Unless you know something about the development of the slave trade, the agricultural practices of the pre–Civil War South, and the Civil War and its aftermath, you can't fully understand current race relations in the U.S. The conflicts in Yugoslavia, Ireland, Kurdistan, and the Middle East cannot be truly understood without a grasp of each region's history. The history of relationships between Mexico and Texas, between China and the U.S., between men and women, between immigrants and citizens, all provide crucial background for appreciating where we are today. And it all touches you. If the United States ever declares war, you or some of your friends may be on the troop planes out. If trade barriers are established with China, the cost of your shoes or your jeans may rise. You may not immediately see how international events touch your life — but they do. As you are sitting in your classes or doing your homework, think, "What is the connection between all of this and me?" There will always be one, and the challenge is for you to find it.

U.S. history focuses on this country. World history focuses on how this country fits into the rest of the world and how past events in other countries helped to shape our present. World geography gives you a window onto the entire world. There is lots of talk today about our "global village." Telecommunications, international trade, and interconnected interests make the world a much smaller place than it was for our grandparents. Those who understand this world are better prepared to live in it.

Many school districts require a course in government. In our democracy, all eligible voters have a chance to express their opinions by choosing the elected officials who make public policy decisions. If you figure out how the system works, lobby your causes, and help elect people who represent your viewpoints, you influence policy. Government class teaches you how this happens.

Many of the decisions that public bodies must make are very complicated, and these decisions affect people for decades to come. Real people like your parents or sister or cousin or boyfriend can suffer the consequences of policy decisions. To understand the scope of an issue, one must learn about culture, history, geography, economics, and politics. Social Studies aims to give you the information and tools to make informed decisions.

It matters to all of us that you participate intelligently in the democratic process. Elections can be won by just a few votes, and those who are elected have the power, sometimes, to change the course of history. Any single person reading this may, one day, affect the lives of hundreds of thousands of people with a single vote and never know it.

Classes to Choose. Good academic preparation includes a minimum of three years of Social Studies. Usually, this encompasses a year of U.S. History and a year of World History or World Geography. Your school may require government and/or economics as well. If there is no requirement, take a U.S. history course, something international, and something that will help you see how government and economics work so you can understand issues related to taxation, trade, social security, and investments.

Physical education/Health. You may change your career several times in your life. You may change the place where you live, maybe even the people you live with. There is only one thing I can assure you will never change during your lifetime: you will live in the same body. Therefore, it makes sense that you take care of it and keep it in good condition. Physical education (P.E.) and health are about giving you exercise and information to care for that body and the skills to enjoy physical activity.

Team sports offer many benefits. Beyond the fun of playing and competing, training develops discipline. We learn how to collaborate by playing on a team. Sports allow us to get to know other students and develop friendships. Even if you are not yet skilled enough to play at the varsity level, join a community team and experience competitive athletics. If you really don't enjoy physical competition, you might want to get involved as a manager or support person. Use these years to find some form of physical activity that you like and can continue after you graduate. Take advantage of health, sex education, or life skills classes to be informed about situations that affect your physical well-being.

Classes to Choose. In addition to standard Physical education classes, ROTC, dance, drill squad, marching band, and cheerleading may count as P.E. credit as well as participation in school sports teams. Many schools require a semester of Health in addition to Physical education.

Check out your local requirements with your counselor. Sometimes P.E. and/or Health can be skipped if you are taking certain work-study classes that require time away from school. Think ahead. If you think you are going to want to do work-study, you may want to skip P.E. classes in your freshman and sophomore years to concentrate on academic requirements. But if you change your mind later, and don't take the courses that exempt you from P.E., you will have to fill in those required P.E. credits in order to graduate.

Foreign languages. While many states do not require any foreign language, learning a second language is part of a first-class high school education. It makes a larger part of the world more easily accessible and understandable to you. For example, 500 million people in the world speak Spanish as their first or second language, and if you can speak it, too, you have a greater ability to communicate for business and pleasure. More and more employers want employees who are multilingual. I took Spanish classes in Mexico a few summers ago and found attorneys, teachers, and business executives all using vacation time to learn Spanish because they were convinced it would benefit them in their work. Many students find that in learning a foreign language, they are helped in their understanding of English and in appreciating the subtle way in which words shape thought and reflect the culture of the country.

While it is a bonus to speak other languages, if you are struggling with math, English, and science, it is more important to take extra classes that can help you with these core academics than to study a second language. If you need time in your schedule for remediation or tutorial work, if you want to pursue another subject that fascinates you or if you need class time for career and technology training, you may need to drop language classes.

There are also enjoyable ways to learn another language outside of school. Consider the possibility of spending a semester, a year, or a summer in a foreign country. Talk with your language teacher or counselor about how to make this happen. Consider taking a year after high school to live in a foreign country and learn the language. Some of the organizations that arrange student travel are American Field Service, World Learning, Youth for Understanding, and Amigos de las Americas. There is some scholarship money available from these and similar organizations. The Council on Standards for International Educational Travel (CSIET) publishes a list of travel and study abroad programs that meet CSIET standards. Send $8.50 to CSIET, 3 Loudoun St. SE, Leesburg, VA 22075 (703-771-2040) for a copy.

Some communities, especially those with large Asian populations, run private Saturday language schools so that students can learn the language and culture of their parents. You might consider paying to attend these special private classes as another way of developing a second language.

> **Classes to Choose.** Although Latin is out of fashion, students with only a year or two in their schedules for language may find this an excellent basis for linguistic understanding because it is the basis of all the romance languages, including English; others may wish to take Latin and a modern language. Otherwise, sign up for the language of your choice and try to take at least three years. In some schools, if a dozen or so students request a language well in advance of the school year, the school must provide a teacher. In other districts, students may be granted a transfer if the school they are attending does not offer a chosen language. Think carefully about which language you'd like to choose. It may seem fun and exotic to learn something unusual, but it's often more practical to speak a widely used language. On the other hand, a love of a particular language, whether or not it is popular, can lead you to the places you want to go.

Fine Arts. Do you enjoy listening to music or making music, going to movies, dancing, drawing, taking pictures, even reading comics? All these activities are rooted in the arts. There is great joy in developing your artistic self. Students who forget history dates or math formulas often find they easily recall arts information. Expressing yourself visually or kinesthetically uses and develops different parts of the brain than thinking with words. Be wide open to experiences that involve looking and moving in new ways. Try out various art forms just for fun. Don't be afraid of not being "good enough." If it gives you pleasure, this is "good enough." Whether or not you become skilled enough to draw or dance, for example, you are likely to enjoy the work of others so much more when you have had a chance to appreciate the process that goes into artistic creation.

A serious immersion in any aspect of the arts will lead you to learning in other disciplines as well — perhaps history, science, or psychology. In order to be creative, you must be well grounded in the technical aspects of your field. In music, for example, you must appreciate the science of sound; in dance, you must master anatomy and kinesthesiology.

Classes to Choose. This subject area embraces visual art, music, theater arts, and dance. Different schools offer different choices, but most high schools have classes in at least two of the four areas. You want to look for exposure to both theory and practice. Art I, for example, usually starts with a foundation in design, drawing and vocabulary, and higher level classes lead to increased exposure and the opportunity for specialization. Music classes include band, orchestra, and choral music. Some schools have a course in the history and literature of an arts area like music or dance. Don't make the mistake of ignoring Fine Arts classes because they seem unacademic — or worse, unmasculine — to you. The arts offer you entrees to both careers and personal pleasures.

Career and Technology courses. Turn to Chapter 12, Using School to Start Your Career, for specific information about preparing for work after high school. When I was a high school student, there was an unfortunate bias that college-bound students took academic classes and "the kids who weren't smart" took vocational classes. Shades of this attitude linger on in some schools, and career counselors sometimes complain that class counselors steer academic students away from career preparation courses and steer work-oriented students away from tough academic classes. However, *everyone* needs basic academics whether or not college is in the picture. And *everyone* benefits from exposure to career planning and skills training, whether they are headed to college or not. You may have noted earlier that in Texas, one credit of a computer course is a state requirement. This career and technology class has been judged so essential to career training that it is now incorporated into every Texas student's schedule.

In order to learn how college admissions officers respond to the tension between career and academic counselors, I called the admissions office of several colleges. At Princeton, I was told that students were judged on the toughest academics. What they took for electives made no difference: yearbook was not considered to be more important than car mechanics; band class was not considered to be more important than heating and air conditioning repair. At Texas A&M, I was told that a student who fulfilled most all the academic requirements by the end of junior year and used senior year to sample career and technology skills would be viewed as less industrious than someone who stayed with traditional academics and, for example, took a second year of physics instead of a first year of health sciences laboratory skills. The admissions director at SMU felt that some college admissions officers did not yet see the full value of well-designed career and technology classes. In summary, high schools are right to urge students to think about career options and take career exploration courses, but colleges do not want students to take these classes *in place* of academics.

For most students, this will not be a problem. Colleges that base admission on test scores, grades, and class standing don't worry about every entry on your transcript. Schools with open admissions or techni-

Reading the Small Print

If there is a special course you want to take and no one can tell you where it is offered, there is probably a **master catalog** for your school district. You can look through it to find out whether there is a course offered at another high school that you cannot find at your own. There should also be a book with a title like *Description of High School Courses* which can be obtained from your counselor or the curriculum department of your school district. It describes what each course is supposed to teach you.

Most large urban school districts print secondary school guidelines that summarize all the high school rules and regulations, but it is usually intended more for staff than students. Your way of finding out this information is to read the handouts you are given and listen to teachers and counselors. Read the materials you are given because the better you understand the rules, regulations, and possibilities, the easier it is to play the game successfully.

cal schools don't care what classes you have taken so long as you are prepared to do their work. This is an issue only for students interested in applying to competitive colleges. Call the admissions office at one of the colleges you are considering and speak to the director or assistant director of admissions if you are not sure what to do.

When You Think What You Are Being Taught Is Wrong It will be surprising if in four years of high school you don't meet at least one teacher with theories and teaching methods that are different from yours or your family's. This can create an interesting learning experience because you will have to think carefully about why you disagree and why you believe what you do.

Remember, ideas are not germs. Being exposed to them does not mean you catch them. Note, for example, that Protestant students attend Catholic schools — and don't become Catholics. Catholic children go to nonsectarian schools and hear views contrary to those of their church, but they don't abandon their church. Republicans marry Democrats but don't switch party loyalty. Hearing and thinking about different ideas in school does not mean you should give up your own ideas. It does mean you should try to figure out *why* people think differently. In many instances, there is not a single right answer but a range of interpretations that result from diverse experiences, assumptions, and interests. Analyzing different interpretations to see how they developed is a wonderful way to learn about yourself and others.

8. Diplomas

High School Diplomas

Different school systems offer their own diploma options, but most of these options fit the general pattern described below.

Students earn:

- a regular or core diploma by meeting the district's standard requirements

- an advanced diploma by meeting a higher set of standards

- an advanced diploma with honors that requires yet even higher standards

- an IEP (Individual Educational Program) diploma for special education students who have left the mainstream program for individually tailored education aimed at preparing them for employment

Usually, these are not different diplomas. Every graduate earns the basic diploma to which seals or ribbons are attached indicating honors, advanced standing or other special levels of recognition. For example, in New York, students take a required set of tests called the Regents exam, named in tribute to the Board of Regents who are appointed by the governor to oversee school policy at the state level. Students who pass the exam at a certain level and have taken additional credits have a Regents' endorsement on their regular diploma. A higher level is the Regents' endorsement with honors.

How do you decide which diploma to work toward? Actually, you start by thinking about things other than a diploma. Your diploma is far less important than the more intangible information and skills you have inside your head when high school is over. Yes, you want that diploma because it is both a symbol of success to others and a necessary requirement to pass on to many other opportunities. *But the really important issue is preparation, not graduation.* Graduation is the end of high school, but it is just the beginning of your adult life. I talked in the first chapter about high school being a foundation. When you graduate, you are ready to begin constructing the life you want on that foundation.

Students should take the courses they need to be prepared to start construction. Here's an example: Suppose a junior is interested in a career in emergency medicine and is aiming to become certified after high school as an emergency medical technician. There are, lucky for her, several career courses in her high school that she should be taking for this. There is also a course at the local community college that fits her plan perfectly and that offers high school credit. But in order to do this, it is going to be impossible to take third-year Spanish because of the way the schedule works out. Yet an honors diploma requires three years of a language, and this student has been aiming for an honors diploma. Since she has a clear plan, it may make more sense to focus on preparing for her career after high school rather than having a gold seal on her diploma. If she feels Spanish language skills are important, she might enroll in an intensive Spanish class at the local university the summer after graduation to compensate for not taking third-year Spanish in high school.

On the other hand, if this young woman is aiming for a highly competitive college and then medical school as preparation for being an emergency room physician, she would be better served to pursue the more stringent academic requirements that will be beneficial in applying to colleges while taking enough career education to confirm that medicine is the right direction for her. She should learn the Spanish now and use the four years of medical school to get the experienced-based skills.

Many school officials have spent a great deal of time figuring out the programs that will prepare you to be competitive and successful in today's world. Schools across the country are rapidly developing "artic-ulated sequences" — year-by-year course schedules that allow students to follow programs that prepare them for both a career and future edu-cation. Look for these plans, often called Tech Prep, in your school.

My advice is to go for the hardest program and the highest level diploma possible without feeling constant stress and struggle. Why? Higher level diplomas are generally more demanding, and the more dif-ficult the school program, the more you are likely to learn. The more you learn, the richer you are for the rest of your life. Higher and harder also puts you up against tougher competition. Better to train to play in a faster game and work harder to score than to do well with no effort in a slower game.

Do *not* take advanced classes because you think that's the thing to do if you're having difficulty and feeling frustrated most of the time. If you need to take remedial classes to fill in holes in your education, do it. Don't let labels, other people's opinions, the actions of your friends, or the common conventions of your school stand in the way of getting the education that is right for you.

The trend nationwide now is to upgrade educational standards, so different grades in your school may have different graduation standards. Don't rely on what you hear from an older brother or sister. Juniors may have one set of requirements and incoming freshmen another. Check out written graduation standards for your year to be sure you know what diploma choices there are for you and what is required to earn each one. These standards may be set by your year of graduation or by the year high school begins — for example, all students who graduate in the year 2000 or later must have . . . , or, all students who enter the ninth grade in 1997 or later must have . . .

Students working at an advanced level may have additional course options as well as degree choices. Most high schools offer Advanced Placement classes, which are high school courses taught at a college level. The College Board offers AP exams in a variety of courses, and students who score high on these exams may be given credit by their colleges. AP courses are typically considered honors-level courses by high schools. In certain school districts students can earn, in addition to the diploma, an International Baccalaureate degree, which is recognized by foreign countries and is considered to be at the advanced level. Plan intelligently. Find out in your freshman year what your choices are.

Special Education students may have modified graduation requirements that are specified in their IEP (Individual Education Plan). An IEP is developed for each special education student. A plan may include waivers for mandated graduation tests. See Chapter 9 for more information about tests, and see Chapter 17, Special Education.

GED: General Educational Development Test

Who Gets a GED? If you do not finish high school, you may take a test that certifies that you have a high school understanding of reading, writing, grammar, math, science, and social studies. If you pass the test, you receive a General Educational Development certificate, commonly known as a GED. It is generally not regarded as favorably as a diploma from an accredited high school.

However, there are times when a GED may be the right choice.

One Teacher's Thoughts on the GED

While talking with a highly skilled welding teacher, I asked about students who might not do so well in academic classes but who might like and be good in a trade. "What if a student gets job skills in your classes but then gets a GED and goes out to work?" I asked.

The teacher looked at me like I was thinking slowly. "The kids who want a GED are usually the lazy ones. If they're lazy going to school, they're lazy going to work. Employers can hire high school graduates. Why should they hire people who are not?" Whether you agree or disagree, this is an opinion many people share.

For adults who could not attend or complete high school, and especially for those who now want to attend college, a GED is an acceptable certificate. If high school is a disaster for you, and you can see no prospects of making it work and are planning to drop out, discuss getting a GED with your counselor so you can move on to on-the-job training or more education in a different setting. If your personal situation makes it difficult to attend high school classes, you may want to take the GED. Migrant students may find this a necessary route but federal law helps migrant students transfer among districts. For students who need to be out of high school and into college, a GED is one way to get there. It is better to have a GED than no diploma. *Please* read about different ways to do high school in Chapter 16 before deciding on this route.

If you are approaching your twenties and not within a year or so of graduation, you might consider a GED certificate. This is worth a serious discussion with your counselor or a respected teacher. But remember that you will benefit your entire life from learning skills. A degree without knowledge is like getting a great bargain on shoes — only to find the shoebox you bring home has only one shoe in it. It doesn't matter that you graduate at twenty-one instead of eighteen if you graduate with knowledge and information in your head that can help you survive and thrive in your life after high school.

What if you receive a GED but decide later you want to go further with your education? Any college with open admissions, including most publicly supported community colleges, will accept students with a GED. The problem is not getting accepted but passing the entry level tests for math and English. If you do not pass these tests, the college will place you in noncredit developmental classes to improve your skills. You will have to pay for and pass the noncredit class before beginning the required for-credit math or English class.

Some statistics suggest that GED students at community colleges do as well as students with conventional high school diplomas. Stephen V. Cameron and James J. Heckman, two economists at the University of Chicago, became interested in the rise in number of students who are taking the GED instead of graduating high school. They decided to look at the causes and consequences of this. In 1993, they published the article "The Nonequivalence of High School Equivalents" in *The Journal of Labor Economics.* They concluded:

> Exam-certified high school equivalents are statistically indistinguishable from high school dropouts. Whatever differences are found among exam-certified equivalents, high school dropouts and high school graduates are accounted for by their years of schooling completed. *There is no cheap substitute for school.*

Although the GED board allows students over sixteen to be given the GED test, state boards of education set their own limits. In many states, you must be eighteen to take the GED. In some states seventeen-year-olds may take the GED if they can honestly sign a statement that they have no contact with their parents, if they bring in proof of marriage or if they have a signed and notarized letter from a parent asking they be given the test. The cost for the test and the certificate of completion varies by testing center. For example, it costs $40 at the Houston Community College and at the testing centers administered by the Los Angeles Public Schools. In Miami, the school district referred me to a testing center that charges $25. In Detroit, the public school system administers tests for $15.

In big cities, the GED test is probably given somewhere every work day of the year. High school counselors and community college admissions staff should know where you can take the test. Often high schools have their own free GED programs for students who are considering dropping out of school. Community groups may also offer you free preparation and testing. Another alternative is the Job Corps, which helps young men and women aged sixteen to twenty-four complete their GEDs and obtain basic job training. For more information, call 1-800-JOB-CORPS.

The GED test is usually given over a two- or three-day period.

There are five parts of the test and you take all five parts in the same testing period.

- Writing Skills: 75 minutes plus 45 minutes for an essay
- Reading Skills: 65 minutes
- Math: 90 minutes
- Science: 95 minutes
- Social Studies: 85 minutes (multiple choice)

You may retake any part you do not pass. With a letter stating you are prepared to retake the section(s) from a certified GED instruction center, you can take the test again after ninety days. Without the letter, you must wait six months. There is a small cost for retaking each section. In 1995, about 63 percent of people who took the GED in the U.S., its territories, and Canada received certificates of completion.

If you have questions about the GED, contact the General Educational Development Testing Service, which is part of the American Council on Education at One Dupont Circle NW, Suite 250, Washington, DC 20036-1163. The hotline information number is 1-800-62-MYGED (626-9433).

9. Tests: Which Ones, When, Why, and How to Do Better

In high school you'll take zillions of tests — from quizzes that count for ten points to tests that determine if you will graduate. This chapter talks about the tests that are especially important — state-required graduation tests, SAT, ACT, class finals, and college competency tests — and why they are important, what they mean, and how you prepare for them. Tests are the hurdles you jump to get through high school. Like a good hurdler, if you put in the time to learn, you'll get over most of them successfully.

Achievement Tests and Aptitude Tests

Achievement tests measure what you have learned in specified subjects. Aptitude tests measure how easily you may be able to learn certain subjects or skills. You may, for example, show a very high aptitude for learning languages even if you have never studied a foreign language.

In the subjects where you have a high aptitude, you'll find it easier to learn the material. In subjects where you have less natural aptitude, you may encounter frustration and need to make a greater effort.

Required State Tests

More and more states require high school students to pass achievement tests to graduate. Students must pass an exit exam to graduate in Alabama, Arkansas (effective '96–'97), Arizona (essential skills test recorded on transcript), Florida, Georgia, Hawaii, Indiana (unless principal certifies student has met Core 40 requirements), Louisiana, Maryland, Massachusetts (must pass proficiencies, but not a single exit exam), Mississippi, Nevada, New Jersey, New Mexico (to graduate with a diploma), New York, North Carolina, Ohio, South Carolina, Tennessee, Texas, and Virginia. Minnesota students graduating in the year 2000 must pass tests in reading, math, and writing to meet the requirements of the Minnesota Graduation Rule. Pennsylvania students must achieve fifty-two state academic performance outcomes plus local outcomes.

There is, however, disagreement about the value of these tests. Some people think these tests focus teachers on the test material and get in the way of thoughtful, stimulating teaching. Others believe that the tests make sure that students learn the basics they need for life after high school. As a student, however, these arguments are moot if you live in a state that requires testing. You simply must pass the test.

Your principal and your teachers may be "graded" by how many students in your school pass the achievement tests. Parents, businesses, and public agencies may use scores to assess the quality of your school. Many people besides you have a lot riding on how well you do on this test. This may mean there is extra help and tutorial sessions available to prepare you for testing. If you need it, use it.

You should ask the following questions about required achievement tests:

- In what grade(s) are the tests given and when?

- What am I expected to know to pass the tests?

- Are there old tests or study tests I can review?

- Is the test timed or can you take as long as you want?

- What happens if I don't pass?

- Can I retake the sections I don't pass, or must I retake the entire test?

- When do I retake sections that I didn't pass?

- Are special tutorial sessions available to me?

Retaking the Test In many cases, state-mandated tests are administered in the spring. If you don't pass all parts of the test, it may be a good idea to go directly to a summer program that is offered for students who have not passed. An advantage of a summer program is that you may be able to retake the test at the end of summer school, when the information is still fresh in your mind.

One high school student told me that she and her friends didn't bother taking their required test in tenth grade when it was first scheduled so they could take the morning off. Now a senior, she has not passed the math section, and she is in a panic. "Students really need to take this and not fool around," she advises. This is good advice.

The SAT and ACT Tests

SAT stands for **Scholastic Assessment Test**, a national college admissions test administered by the College Board. The **ACT**, the **American College for Testing**, also administers a national admissions test. Many colleges use one or the other of these tests as part of their admissions process. Both are scheduled for selected Saturday mornings at various high school and college testing centers throughout the country and in foreign countries. (Students who for religious reasons cannot take the test on Saturday morning may take it the next day, on Sunday. Read the instructions in the registration form.) Approximately 1 million students take the tests each year.

The **SAT I** is a three-hour test. It is divided into two sections, verbal and mathematical. The verbal section assesses how well you understand what you read (your reading comprehension) and your vocabulary level. The mathematical section measures arithmetical reasoning and algebra and geometry comprehension. The math facts and formulas that you need to solve the problems are provided in the test booklet. You take both sections on the same day.

The **ACT** test aims to assess your general educational development and your aptitude for completing college-level work. It includes evaluation in four subject areas: reading, English, mathematics, and science reasoning. This test is given on Saturday mornings from 8 A.M. to 12:15 P.M. Like the SAT, there is a Sunday morning option.

Some high schools prefer that students take the SAT. Others favor the ACT. Many college counselors advise students to take both. While each test is designed to predict success in college, they are organized differently. The SAT subtracts points for wrong answers, so you must develop a strategy for when to guess on questions you are not sure about. The ACT doesn't penalize for the wrong answer, but the ACT puts more emphasis on reading comprehension skills. If you don't know which tests to take, talk with your college counselor and/or the admissions officers at the colleges you are considering.

One good feature of the ACT is that you can control which scores are sent where. When you register for the test, you may direct your scores to be sent to selected colleges by filling in the college codes from the registration booklet. If you do not put in any college codes, scores will be sent only to your home address. If you retake the test and again include no codes, you can choose which set of scores you want to report to colleges. The College Board will send all scores.

Fee Waivers If you cannot afford the test fee, talk with your counselor. Counselors can provide income-eligible students with a form to return with the registration for either test that allows you to test at no cost. No student need skip college admissions tests for lack of money.

When to Register The registration deadline for these tests is about six weeks before the test (check the deadlines in the test information materials). I encourage you to register eight to ten weeks ahead of time. When you register, you request which testing center you want to use. If the center you prefer has already filled, you will be assigned to a different location, which may be less convenient. Your guidance office will have SAT and ACT bulletins that tell you how to register and give you other useful facts about the test. Pick up a bulletin, read that small print and share it with your parents.

If you forget to register on time, all may not be lost. You can apply a week or so late and pay the late fee of $15 or $20. If you are really late but desperate to take a certain test, the SAT offers standby registration for $30. Go to the test center *early* the day of the test as a standby; if space is available, you may take the test. Standby registration is not available for the ACT.

Sophomore- and Junior-Year Practice Practice makes perfect. It is a good idea to practice taking the tests before your scores count for college admissions. **Take a practice test in your sophomore year** so you can see where you are already strong, where you need to concentrate your studying efforts, and how you can improve your test-taking skills.

If you think you'll be taking the ACT, take ACT's PLAN in your sophomore year. This test is designed specifically for sophomores and is scored so you know where you stand compared to other test-takers at the tenth grade level. It is a three-hour test and costs $7.75.

If you plan to take the SAT I, take the PSAT (Preliminary Scholastic Assessment Test) in your sophomore year. This is a two-hour version of the three-hour SAT I. The PSAT is designed for juniors and is used to determine National Merit Scholars, a College Board scholarship program. It costs $8.50, and scores will *not* be sent to colleges. With your scores, you will get a customized report of your performance, item by item, and a copy of your actual test booklet. You will also get a predicted SAT I score for the SAT. You can compare your tenth grade PSAT score with scores of others who have taken the test who will be mostly eleventh graders.

When you are taking the SAT I and/or ACT tests, you register directly with the testing agency using the registration booklets that are available in most every counselor's office. PSAT and PLAN are different. There is a separate booklet that you get from your counselor, and you register through your school. Each test is only given once a year, usually in the third week of October and usually in your school during the school day. So, as soon as you get back to school in the fall, sign up and put it on your calendar. If you miss the PSAT or PLAN tests in your sophomore year and still want to take a practice test, you may sign up for the regular ACT or SAT I, which are usually given in October, November, December, January, March, May, and June. If you have questions that the registration book doesn't answer for you, call the College Board directly at 1-800-999-9139 in Princeton, New Jersey, or ACT at (319) 337-1270 in Iowa City, Iowa.

An advantage of taking practice tests in your sophomore and/or junior year is that it puts you in the college information pipeline. Colleges will send you information, which can help you in your decision-making process, if you indicate on your registration that you would like your name released for this purpose. You can use your scores to target colleges with freshman class scores in your range.

If you think you are college-bound, you'll certainly want to take the PSAT in *October of your junior year*. This is the test that the three major national scholarship programs — National Merit Scholarships, National Achievement Awards for Outstanding Negro Students, and National Hispanic Scholars Recognition Program — use to award merit scholarships.

Understand that even if you take the PSAT or PLAN, you still must take the SAT I or the ACT if you are applying to colleges or universities which require these tests. Even if your prospective colleges do not require test scores, SAT or ACT scores can be helpful in course placement in college. A good time to take the SAT or the ACT is the spring of your junior year. If you are not satisfied with your scores, you may take the test again in the fall of your senior year.

SAT Subject Tests The SAT II Subject Tests, formerly SAT Achievement Tests, are one-hour end-of-course exams that measure your knowledge in specific subject areas. You may take SAT II subject tests in English Composition (with or without an essay), Literature, American History and Social Studies, European History and World Cultures, Mathematics Level I, Mathematics Level II, Spanish, French, German, Hebrew, Latin, Biology, Chemistry, and Physics. Many colleges do not require any achievement test, but highly academic, competitive schools usually want to see your scores from three subject tests.

The best time to take these tests is when the information is fresh in your mind. If you want to test in chemistry and you take the class your sophomore year, take the chemistry subject test in May or June of that year. If you've studied Spanish through your junior year but don't plan to take Spanish your senior year, take that test junior year. Your test fee is reduced if you take three tests at one time, but you are likely to get better scores if you take each of the three tests when the material is fresh and most complete in your mind. Once the scores are reported to you, they will be included in any scores you ask to be sent to colleges. Read the registration book for more information.

Some schools use subject test scores to place students in college classes or allow students to receive college credits. You will want to investigate the credit-by-exam policy at the colleges you are considering.

Preparing for College Tests The best way to prepare for these tests is to read at least thirty minutes a day from elementary school onward. Vocabulary and reading comprehension are hard to study at the last minute because they develop over time. However, if you increase the amount of time you spend reading right now, you may make a difference. Work on learning new vocabulary words. The vocabulary words your English teachers have been assigning might appear on the SAT I or ACT. If you memorize only the meaning of a word for a class test and never use the word or see it in reading, you are not likely to remember it. Get your friends to make a game of playing with these words, of intentionally using them in casual conversation. Instead of ragging your buddy with "You're such a slob," tell him he is "slovenly," "indiscriminate," "unkempt," or "reprehensible." To prepare for the math test, review basic concepts. The SAT I math test does not include advanced math beyond Algebra I and geometry.

Ask your counselor if your school offers SAT prep classes. Many schools have free preparatory sessions on weekends or after school. Some students take a course offered by private businesses to prepare for the SAT. While many teens find these private courses helpful, they can be costly. An alternative is to read books like the Princeton Review's *Cracking the SAT*, which offers helpful test-taking information. Or buy other study guides and books of practice tests. There are also computer programs that provide test review and practice. Don't wait until a week before the test to begin preparing. The summer is a good time to take practice tests. Use your results to review. Spend at least twenty minutes each day reviewing. If you find this difficult, stop after twenty minutes, but make yourself spend that little bit of time every day.

The following test-taking tips will likely help you:

- Get a good night's rest before the test and allow plenty of time to get to the test so you don't arrive rushed and anxious.

- Eat before you go. If you get hungry during the three hours of test-taking, it will be harder to concentrate.

- Take a snack with you. You are not permitted to eat during the test, but there will be a break during which you will be allowed to eat.

- Wear comfortable clothes. Take a sweater or sweatshirt in case the testing center is chilly.

- Resist stress. Everyone passes this test, and getting tense only makes doing the work more difficult. If you feel anxious during the test, stop for a minute and take some very deep breaths with your eyes shut and your body relaxed.

Remember, the SAT or ACT is just one test, and you can't fail it. Your score does not determine whether you go to college or not. It only helps you and the colleges decide at which school you are most likely to do well. While the highly academic colleges take mostly students with higher test scores, there are many fine colleges that take students without regard to what they score. Your score will help you select the best place for you.

How to Read Your Test Scores

Reading test scores can be confusing. Here are some basics.

ACT. The most important ACT score is the composite score — the sum of all four tests. This score can be as low as 1 and as high as 35. About two thirds of the students who take the test fall between 12 and 24. With less than a 17, your college options will be limited; with more than a 27, you will be competitive anywhere. The mean (the point at which half the test-takers scored higher and half scored lower) composite score for college-bound high school students is approximately 18.

SAT. SAT scores range between 200 and 800 for each section of the test. The mean verbal score is 500; the mean math score is 504. Scores below 400 limit college choices. Scores in the 600s and above increase your post–high school options. In 1995, the SAT scores were recentered and you cannot compare the old scores with new ones without an adjustment. Recentering was an adjustment to return the statistical mean of those taking the test to 500. Older scores, before recentering, will convert to high scores on the recentered scale. You are measured, however, against those taking the test at the same time as you.

The College Board reports that when seniors who first took the SAT test as juniors repeated the test, 55 percent improved their scores, 35 percent had lower scores, and 10 percent had no change. On average, the verbal scores improved 13 points, the math scores 10 points. About 1 in 25 students gained 100 or more points on the verbal or math tests. The College Board also reports that the higher a student's scores as a junior, the less likely that subsequent scores will be higher, and the lower the scores, the more likely that subsequent scores will be higher.

SAT II Subject Tests. Each subject test has its own scoring pattern. The mean or middle score may be different for each test you take, but in general, the subject means are in the high 500s or low 600s, with the exception of the German (with listening) test, for which the mean is 535.

When you take a subject test and request that the score be sent directly to a college, the College Board will send all scores from all SAT I and II tests with the exception of subject scores you have placed on hold. Most schools use your highest scores or an average of scores from taking the test more than once. If you become ill or panicked during a test, be sure to cancel your scores. Don't just leave the test in the middle. Talk to the person in charge, explain you are ill, ask to cancel your scores and ask for a ticket to register for another test. Anyone may put a hold on test scores within three days of taking the test. If you do this, you don't get the scores and neither do colleges.

College Skills Tests

Colleges that don't use ACT or SAT tests as a part of admissions are likely to have their own entry tests to help determine your readiness for college work. Many community colleges insist you score at a certain level in reading, English, and math in order to begin college credit courses. If you don't achieve that score, you enroll in developmental classes designed to help bring you up to college level. You will pay for these developmental courses but you will not be earning college credit. These classes offer students a chance to make up for past mistakes and get back on track academically.

It makes much more sense, however, to learn this material for free in high school and begin earning credits toward college graduation right away. Usually these tests apply only to students aiming for a two year associate's degree. If you want to enroll in a short-term certificate program for a specific career, you may not need to worry about passing these tests — but you should worry about what you don't know if you haven't mastered the material covered on the tests. You may want to enroll in a developmental class even if the community college does not require it for your program.

Finals

Every semester you face final exams. The purpose of the final is as much to help you take permanent ownership of what you learned during the semester as to determine your grade. You hardly need this book to tell you that if you keep up during the semester, you'll be in better shape to take your finals. If you fall behind, you're in trouble. But if you have

---

Ways to Make Getting Ready for Finals Easier

- Don't wait until the night before the test to study. Your brain keeps learning while you sleep. If you start reviewing for finals a few days, even a week, ahead of time, your brain will work on mastering the material even when you are not thinking about it.
- Keep your class notes, class handouts, homework assignments, and old tests organized throughout the semester. These are terrific study materials. What your teacher talks about in class is what he or she considers important, so take good notes and review this material for the final.
- Don't mistake thinking about studying, talking about studying, sitting in front of your books talking on the phone, or daydreaming for studying. Sometimes, students believe they have put time into preparing for finals when very little of that time actually went into real studying.

---

been neglectful of a subject during the semester, it may still be possible to make up some lost ground.

As you approach finals, put everything but schoolwork aside for ten days, develop a study schedule, and focus on reviewing. Chapter 10 gives you ideas on how to study effectively.

Testing for Learning Problems

In sports, it is usually easy to see who is coordinated and who isn't. It is not always easy, however, to figure out whose wiring makes reading, writing and manipulating numbers difficult for them.

Many students have one or another kind of learning difficulties. Some are easily seen, but many are not obvious and require testing to identify and treat. A learning problem will give you less trouble if we can name the problem, describe it, and then use what is known about it to help you get around it.

All competent schools want to give every student the kind of learning support he or she needs to do well, and many schools have excellent resources for students. Sometimes, though, need overtakes the resources. A district may want to offer every student what he or she needs, but schools don't always hit the bull's-eye. If your school system is not working for you, keep working for yourself, keep looking for the kind of help you need so you can learn.

Trust your instincts about yourself. If you've been working very hard but with little success and think you may have a learning disability, talk with your counselor. You may want to bring in a family member who can ask for diagnostic testing to determine your problem. If you don't feel heard by your counselor or teacher, it's O.K. to talk to the assistant principal or, if necessary, the principal. Explain that you are serious about figuring out why you are having difficulty in spite of making a great effort. The better you can explain what happens to you when you are studying and what kind of trouble you are having, the more people can help you.

If your school believes you may have a learning disability, it will test you for free. Testing for learning problems is also available from many private sources, but it is expensive. To learn more about learning disabilities, teens or parents can contact the Learning Disability Association of America, 4156 Library Rd., Pittsburgh, PA 15234. Phone: (412) 341-1515. Fax: (412) 344-0224.

See Chapter 15, Special Education, for more information.

Language Proficiency Assessment Testing

When English Is Difficult If you don't know much English, most schools offer bilingual education or special English classes. School districts usually have written policies regarding which students are selected for Limited English Proficiency (LEP) classes. In big districts with many new immigrants, there is a chance, however, that the policy and the reality don't exactly match. English as a Second-Language (ESL) classes may be larger than mandated. Students may find a shortage of teachers or class levels. If the school district is not well organized to help, students must become very assertive in finding what they need. Computers can be a big help. Ask your school to help you use an ESL computer program and insist you get enough time working on the program. You will have to work with your counselor on what "enough" is. See the section If You Think You Have a Small Vocabulary, on pages 103–104, for more ideas on how to learn more words.

In one school district, for example, a score in the 40th percentile of the standard English tests means you don't qualify for LEP assistance. The truth is that if you're scoring below 50 percent, you can benefit from extra work — and if you can make yourself do it, you'll be glad in the long run.

If you are having a great deal of trouble understanding your teachers and your English speaking classmates, you need to ask for help from your counselor.

10. What Does It Mean to Be "Smart" and How Do You Get Smarter?

Use this chapter to understand how people learn and why some learning comes easily while mastering other subjects is difficult — without regard to how "bright" you are.

Howard Gardner, a Harvard University professor, has spent his life studying and writing about how people learn. He believes that there are different kinds of intelligence, meaning that you can be very quick in some subject areas and slower in others.

I, for example, do well on written tests. Speaking and writing come easily to me, but I have zero musical intelligence. I cannot carry a tune or recognize songs. If schools valued musical ability over reading and writing, I would be a dreadful student. When it comes to putting things together, like equipment or puzzles, it takes me a great deal of time and effort to get it right. High school students who have good mechanical or musical intelligence — including many with bad grades and plans to drop out — are much "smarter" than I am in these areas. Does that mean I am dumb? Of course not. We are, each of us, "smart" in different ways.

Different Kinds of Intelligence

Dr. Gardner describes seven kinds of intelligence or ways of knowing. Look through these and think about your own strengths.

1. *Linguistic intelligence.* You like words, whether talking or reading. You learn best with the traditional methods used in school — reading or hearing concepts explained to you — and it is a good bet you do well in school. You are talkative, you learned to read early and you don't mind putting your thoughts down on paper.

2. *Logical-mathematical intelligence.* You are interested in "how?" questions. You like to analyze situations and find the patterns and rules that make things work. People with logical-mathematical intelligence are good with numbers, like calculating things and want to know why things work the way they do. You may like strategy games like checkers or chess and prefer to read instruction manuals rather than novels.

3. *Spatial intelligence.* It is easy for you to think in pictures and you like to understand things by experiencing them either in fact or in your mind's eye. You may like to draw or paint or doodle. You probably enjoyed building blocks as a kid and now enjoy taking things apart or inventing things. When you describe things, you often use visual terms.

4. *Musical Intelligence.* You hear more than other people. You easily pick up rhythms and interesting sound patterns. You have an ear for pitch and melody. You may make music or just like to listen and talk about it. Sometimes you miss the messages people are trying to deliver with words because you are distracted by the sound of the words.

5. *Bodily-kinesthetic intelligence.* Sitting all day in school is hard for you. You want — you *need* — to move. Maybe you are good in athletics or maybe you express your ability by working with your hands on artistic or mechanical projects. The more your body is engaged in learning, the better you learn.

6. *Interpersonal intelligence.* You shine when you are part of a group. You pick up accurately on the feelings of others and understand

their moods and motivations. You can use this gift in different ways. You may be the ringleader, egging others on to action, or you may be a peacemaker who promotes harmony; you might be leading a street gang or you might be president of the student council — it's the same talent.

7. *Intrapersonal intelligence.* Unlike the person with interpersonal intelligence, you prefer to work independently. You have a strong sense of self, and you are quite happy coming up with your own ideas and working on them. Others don't need to tell you what to do because you are busy figuring out things to do on your own.

Linguistic intelligence is the intelligence tested most often in school and measured in work situations. So all students have to figure out how to deal with written tests. But after that, you want to position yourself so you can use your most preferred ways of knowing in the world.

Some people have well-developed intelligence in several areas; others are especially strong in one area. Whatever we have is what we must use. Don't think you lack smarts because linguistic intelligence is not your greatest strength. Accept that linguistic talent is an advantage in school — and then figure out how to make your strengths work for you. Look for school programs and projects that let you draw on your strengths.

Once you understand your own learning style, you can figure out ways to study that work especially for you. For example, if you have high kinesthetic intelligence, you ought to dance yourself into learning your Spanish verbs or your algebra rules. Put on a tape, grab your study sheet, shout that rule out loud, and dance it right into your body. Teens with spatial intelligence may want to put information and concepts into picture form; students with musical intelligence should find ways to give rhythm to what they need to learn.

If you allow yourself to get caught in the "I can't" trap, you are walking into a wall which, really, you could walk around.

If You Have Voices in Your Head That Say "I Can't . . ."

I am writing this book on a computer. Many years ago, I went to work for a consulting company. Everyone in the office wrote reports directly on the computer. I knew nothing about computers then, and those first weeks were awful. I found myself thinking, "I can't do this." And the more I thought that way, the more difficult it was to learn. Finally, I went to my boss and explained that I just couldn't learn to use the computer.

He responded very simply: "If you can't use the computer, you can't work here." In about one minute, the "I can't" of "I can't lose my job" became much more important than the "I can't" of "I can't use a computer." I quickly began saying to myself, "You have got to learn this." Of course, I learned — and it wasn't so hard once I shifted my energies from resisting to succeeding.

Whenever you hear that voice in your head saying "I can't," talk back to it: "Don't tell me 'I can't.' Talk to me about how I can." Most high school students can learn everything they need to learn to graduate — and they can learn tons of stuff they think is not for them. Teenagers no more capable than you are learning material every day you may have written off — because they have decided they must.

After talking with hundreds of teens about what they can and cannot learn, here is what seems true: Mostly, students "can't" learn because they don't believe it is important for them to learn. A high school senior who failed five classes before he "got it together" explains how hard it is to hear the truth: "A lot of people tried to tell me stuff, but I didn't listen. I didn't think I really needed school. I could get a job without it. . . . When I got close enough to see myself graduating, I decided I needed to get my act together."

How Badly Do You Want Success?

I once knew a student who started off in high school poorly. When we met, Junior was in danger of failing many of his ninth grade classes. This seemed odd because it was clear that he was intelligent. One day he said to me, "Dr. Lieberman, you are very smart, and if you are smart and you think I am smart, maybe I am smart."

But this didn't mean his classes suddenly got easier and he got A's. Junior was smart, finally he knew it, but he was still uneducated. He had never done his homework or paid much attention in school, so he didn't know anything — and that made it almost impossible to do high school work. Smart is not enough. In fact, smart is not so important. What counts most is desire and determination.

If you've managed to avoid learning much in elementary school or middle school, it will be difficult to do well in high school. It is not too late to decide you are on the wrong course and change — but time is running out, and so get yourself turned around quickly.

The most important thing this book can do for you is to have you think about success at school as a way to get what you want and need in this world. When you believe that graduating from high school and learning enough to function effectively in the world is your key to building a successful adult life, you will have your head in the right place to do what you need to do.

Desire and Determination Make You Smarter What makes teens most able to improve their school performance is *desire* and *determination*. For all kinds of students with all kinds of backgrounds and abilities, it is clear that **desire** is the key. **Determination** turns desire into reality.

Those who can see success — who want it, taste it, need it — are the ones who find the determination and drive to learn and succeed.

Slow and Steady Works Just Fine

Do you know the story about the hare and the tortoise? The fast hare was so sure he could win a race against the slow tortoise that the hare stopped, far ahead in the race, to rest, and fell asleep. The tortoise, one small step at a time, kept at the race and won. You don't have to be a fast-charging hare to get where you are going. You can get there just the same by taking small steps, so long as you know where you are headed and keep taking those small steps forward. In fact, if you set your goal too great, you may get discouraged. Set a small goal that you know you can reach. When you get there, set another small goal and just keep going like the tortoise.

Teachers can help you read better, grasp math concepts, understand history, unravel a foreign language, and decode science. They cannot drop a determination pill in your body. You have to do that yourself.

Studying Often students tell me that they have studied for tests and still do poorly. What becomes clear in talking with some of these students is that, in fact, they don't know how to study. If you dig a ditch with a teaspoon, it will take much longer than if you use a good shovel. If you don't practice good study habits, it's as if you're using a teaspoon.

Telling you all the things you can do to study effectively would result in a separate book, but here are a few tried and true study strategies. You can learn to be a good student just as you can learn to be a good athlete or good cook.

1. *Be truthful.* Don't lie to yourself. You know when you are studying and when you are pretending, when you are serious and when you are kidding.

2. *Set small goals.* Set small, specific goals. Don't say, "I will work harder on my science." Instead say, "I will memorize the steps of

Study-Skills Books

These four books give you all the strategies and tips you need to develop effective study skills and organize your time so that you are efficient when you study. Your local bookstore can order a book for you, you can contact the publisher directly, or you can browse the bookstore or library shelves to see if something in stock suits you.

Fry, Ron. *Ron Fry's How to Study.* Hawthorne, NJ: Career Press, 1994. *Ron Fry's How to Study* is part of a series of self-help books for students written by Mr. Fry. In addition to advice on organizing yourself for studying effectively, this book has recommendations on how to write class papers, how to participate in class, and how to remember what you read. It costs $9.95.

Kornhauser, Arthur W. *How To Study: Suggestions for High School and College Students.* Rev. ed. Chicago: University of Chicago Press, 1993. *How to Study* is a tiny book — only fifty-one pages. It isn't cute. It doesn't have pictures. It just tells you in a very straightforward way what successful students do and how you can do it too. The book costs $4.95.

continued on next page

photosynthesis or the list of chemical symbols by Tuesday at 7 P.M." Don't say to yourself, "I will *try* . . ." Say instead, "I *am* going to do such and such."

3. *Be organized.* Keep your school papers organized. If you do this, you will have class notes and past tests to study. Figure out a system that works for you and stay organized. It is much less stressful to have a place where everything goes so you know where you can find it. If you are not using a school planner or date book, give it a try. Many students find this helps a great deal in tracking what needs to be done and when.

McCutcheon, Randall J. *Get Off My Brain: A Survival Guide for Lazy Students*. Minneapolis, MN: Free Spirit Press, 1985. The author of this book knows enough about high school students to have been awarded Teacher of the Year for the State of Nebraska in 1985. A quick look at this book may leave you thinking this is a guide on how to sneak by and study little. In fact, McCutcheon's tongue-in-cheek approach delivers lots of good advice with a smile. The book costs $8.95.

Stowers, John C., Jr. *Straight A's: If I Can Do It, So Can You*. New York: McGraw-Hill, 1996. The author of this book describes himself as a mediocre high school student who, after a four-year hiatus, went off to college and immediately discovered he was spending more time on studying and achieving less success than many of his classmates. He decided to figure out their secrets — and graduated with nearly a straight A average. He describes what he learned in these 140 pages. Stowers wrote his book for college students, and I highly recommend it to any college-bound senior, but I also recommend it to high school students who are doing well but wish to improve. The print is small and there isn't lots of white space or cute illustrations to break up the text, but it is well written, easy to read, and full of excellent, sensible advice.

4. *Review.* Go over old homework and do practice problems or exercises. Focus especially on things that gave you trouble the first time around.

5. *Flash cards.* For English or foreign language vocabulary, make flash cards with a word you need to learn on one side and the meaning on the other. Quiz yourself over and over until you know the meanings and definitions well. You can also make flash cards for other subjects. Put a question to yourself on one side and the answer on the other. Again, quiz yourself or get a parent or friend to use your cards and quiz you.

6. *Start early.* Don't wait until the last minute to review for tests or prepare for oral reports. The more nights your brain has to process the information, the better you will remember it.

7. *Look at headings.* Review the chapter(s) you were assigned by reading only the headings and bold-faced captions first. To prepare for a final exam, make an outline of the material you think you need to study from these headings.

8. *Use memory tricks.* Make up songs, sayings, poems, pictures, equations, or silly words that help you remember. For example, many people recall which way to turn their clocks when daylight savings time begins with the saying, "Spring forward, fall back." If you must remember, say, the steps of photosynthesis, make up a silly sentence with the first letter of each word standing for one of the steps.

When you have a choice about project assignments in school, try to do the project in a way that suits your learning style. Suppose the class is studying the Civil War. If you like to learn things in order, like to know the story behind something, then you might choose to do an essay or narrative about events leading up to the war. But if you like to think about things quantitatively — if you're comfortable with numeric reasoning — look for a topic that allows you to use numbers. Maybe you will compare the troop size for different states and the inequalities in numeric strength in battle.

If you like big questions, abstract kinds of things, then you want to choose that kind of question for your project. Maybe you'll look into the nature of slavery and why and how people can accept the roles of slave or master and how that played itself out specifically in the South in the nineteenth century.

If you are a person drawn to the arts, you may enjoy doing your project on, say, Civil War music and how the music and lyrics of the South and the North reflected their views of the war. Or maybe you want to do a series of sketches to accompany a report on some aspect of the war. If none of these approaches appeals to you, you may be a hands-on person who learns best by touching and feeling materials. If that's the case for you, you might choose to create a model of a major Civil War battle. Any of these ways will teach you a great deal about the Civil War, about studying history, developing research skills and completing tasks. So choose ways of working in school, when you can, that make sense for who you are. When you must work in ways that are less pleasing for you, put a positive spin on the situation: understand that you are getting a window on a different way of thinking and learning.

If You Think You Have a Small Vocabulary, Read This Find the very best student you know and try to teach this person something easy — how to scramble an egg for example. But as you teach this task, speak some of the important words in your explanation — like "crack," "melt," and "scramble" — in a foreign language. Even this excellent student will not understand your description of how to scramble the egg if he or she cannot understand enough of the words you use. If you are not understanding many of the English words in class, you are facing the same problem. You may think you are a poor student when the real problem is that you have a limited vocabulary.

Help yourself in the classroom and in the workplace by learning more words. The greater your vocabulary, the better your chance of finding success. Here are ways to build a bigger vocabulary:

- Watch news shows in English or watch a public affairs channel like C-Span, where the vocabulary is not always simple.

- Listen to English talk radio. National Public Radio, for example, has two news shows, *Morning Edition* in the morning and *All Things Considered* in the late afternoon, which use good vocabulary and sentence structure and can help you build your vocabulary.

- Read the newspaper every day.

- Ask people to explain words you don't know, and then try to use those words five or six times more that day. Don't worry about how smart you are. You aren't going to grow more brains! Worry instead about what you're doing with the brain you have already.

Sometimes highly intelligent people become lazy because things come easily, and they end up less successful than those who have learned to work hard. Drive and determination are more important than high IQ numbers. Test this by thinking about successful people you admire. Jot down on a piece of paper ten characteristics that you think contributed to their success. How many of these have to do with aptitude — and how many with attitude? In my own experience, I have come to believe attitude is the more important ingredient.

11. What to Do When Classes Aren't Going Well

If you've ever failed a class or believe you might fail a class, this chapter is for you.

A question: if one hundred people that you respect — including your favorite athlete, your favorite movie star, your favorite teacher, your mother, the president of the United States, and Michael Jordan — all agreed on something, would you listen?

Well, all these people *do* agree on one thing: *don't fail your classes!* You may say, "I don't care. It doesn't matter to me." You are most likely deceiving yourself. Failing doesn't feel good, and once you start feeling badly about yourself and school, it's all too easy to slip into a downward spiral. You lose your spirit, stop trying, and have more disappointments. This is not a good path for anybody to follow.

Fighting Failure

Why do students fail? Most students who fail a class don't have to fail.

The ten most common reasons students use to explain failing are:

1. I was lazy.
2. There was too much work, and I didn't have time.
3. I didn't like the teacher.
4. It didn't seem important.
5. I still had middle school habits.

Teens Talk About Failing

I asked forty high school students if they had ever failed a class because they couldn't understand the work. Not one person felt this was the real reason students fail. Perla Rodriguez explained,

> I failed one class because I thought the course was too difficult, but now I understand that when the class is hard, the only thing to do is work much harder.

Jeff Davis and Sergio Ochoa, two seniors, had similar advice. Jeff said,

> I didn't want to do work. I just wanted to play around . . . Now I wish I wouldn't have been that way. I wish I had paid more attention to schoolwork. Yeah, I am going to graduate, but I have to pass everything this year, and that's pressure. And the only college I'm going to be accepted at is a community college, and now I wish I had a choice.

Jeff nudged Sergio and said, "Sergio was the same way." Sergio shrugged and said,

> I was just trying to fit in. But it wasn't worth it. Later on you realize school is the most important thing. You won't always have your friends, but you can always have your education.

6. I was working at my job and didn't have the time (or energy) for schoolwork at night.
7. I was worried about other problems and couldn't concentrate.
8. I was a full-time mother and didn't have time.
9. The teacher was not a good teacher.
10. I missed too many days of class.

Skip the excuses. In four years of high school, you won't like every teacher or every class. But do the work, figure out something in the class that you can find interesting, take care of yourself by learning something useful from this experience, and get on with it. *You don't have to like it. You do have to do it.* Cut the excuses. Figure it this way: doing things you don't much like now builds discipline muscles. These muscles turn out to be extremely valuable in the adult world.

Your Home Life If bad stuff is happening at home, this can distract you and make school more difficult. Some students have confided that they worry about being sexually abused, about family members being killed, about not having any food, about being beat up, about being evicted, and about their parents or themselves dying. These kinds of worries absolutely get in the way of schoolwork. And they are too great for any one teen or adult to handle alone.

Find an adult — a counselor, a social worker, a person at your place of worship — to share the burden with you. Let them help you find a way to ease your pain. You must free up the energy you need to learn

---

Family Problems

A young woman said to me, "I care more about my family than I care about my grades, and my family is so messed up that I spend all my time trying to make things better."

However, she then explained that all that trying wasn't doing much good.

The best way she can help her mother and brothers and sisters is by getting a good education herself so she can find a satisfying career. Sometimes, you have to put a bubble around yourself and keep the bad situation at bay until you are strong enough and successful enough to leave it behind or help fix it.

---

enough to build the good life you deserve. Even if talking is hard for you, find someone who helps to make it easier. Get involved in sports or other activities that you enjoy to help you relax. *If you are unhappy with the life you have, education is your best way to a better life.*

It's the Teacher's Fault Some students explain that they are not doing well because the teacher is unfair or prejudiced. Others believe that a teacher doesn't like them personally. Some high schoolers quit going to class or doing their homework when they are angry at the teacher.

What if athletes quit the game whenever the umpire made a bad call? What if every time a student was unfair or rude to a teacher, the teacher decided not to show up or to quit teaching for the day? I can hear you saying, "A teacher can't do that. It's the teacher's job to teach." You're right. But it's *your* job to be a student. You can't quit studying every time things don't go right for you, even if you are right and the teacher is wrong. If high school is about doing what is good for you, then walking away is *not* what you want to do because it isn't good for *you*.

What if you are doing the homework and spending extra time trying to figure things out, and things still aren't going well? If you can figure out why your efforts aren't paying off, you may be able to correct the situation. Maybe you need glasses or have a hearing problem. Maybe you have a learning disability — a result of the way your brain is wired. This can make learning certain material especially difficult. Maybe you didn't learn pieces of information along the way that you need in order to do your work now. Could it be a vocabulary problem or your study habits? See the section Testing for Learning Problems in Chapter 9 for more information. It will also help you to read Chapter 10.

When Trying Is Not Enough

Here are some specific things you can do that frequently help students improve their grades and their spirits.

Talk with your teacher. Make an appointment to talk with your teacher when both of you have time for a real conversation. Explain that you are really trying in this class but still have difficulty. Ask the teacher if he or she can determine the reasons for your difficulty and suggest some things to do to help you do better. *Listen* hard to the answer and be willing to try new strategies.

Spend more time on your schoolwork. Sometimes you have trouble in a subject because you are not spending enough time on it. The very subjects that come the hardest are usually the ones that require more of our time than we want to give. For a while, you may need to set aside an hour or two every day to work on just one subject until you begin to figure out how to do it better. Concentrating hard on something day after day usually yields good results.

Find a tutor. If you can afford it, hire a tutor. Someone who is experienced in teaching is the best choice, but if you cannot afford this, consider finding a student who is excellent in the area where you need help — your teacher may be able to suggest someone — and offer to pay that person to meet with you twice a week. If paying money is out of the question, look for a student or adult who will work with you for free. Many schools have tutorial sessions and/or students in the National Honor Society who do this. You may know an adult, perhaps even the parent of a friend or a member of your religious group, who can help you learn the material you find difficult.

Something to remember when asking someone for help: if you show a strong interest, people will be more willing to spend time with you. Push to arrange a regular time to get help. Make sure you show up, and let the person who is helping know you care and appreciate the effort.

Find a study guide. Go to the school library or a local bookstore to find a study guide for the subject that is troubling you. Start at the front of the book and work your way through it, spending a set amount of time on it every day. As soon as you hit a spot where you have trouble, go to work figuring out what it is you don't understand and keep working at it until you do. Ask your teacher for time before or after school for extra help. If you skip what you don't understand, there is a good chance that you'll be tripped up later on.

Do review work. If necessary, go back and take a course over that you passed but in which you didn't learn what you need to know to move ahead. Or ask if there is a review class in school that can help you. Don't be too proud or embarrassed. Be smart enough to do whatever it takes to learn what you need so that you can avoid school failures.

Form a study group. If you know that you learn best in groups, see if you can get a few friends to form a study group. Meet once or twice a week to study together and help each other.

Find emotional support. If personal problems are getting in your way, get help handling them so they don't hurt you first at home and again at school. Find an adult you trust and talk about your problems. See Chapter 20, Solving Problems.

How Much Time Should You Spend on Homework? Just how much time do you spend on homework each week? If the answer is less than ten hours, your problem is *you*. School is your *job* for now — you are supposed to *work* at it.

Some students report spending no more than one hour a school night on homework — often less. Successful high school students who are mastering the material and getting good grades can easily spend ten of fifteen hours a week on homework. If you figure just two hours a night on school nights — that's usually less than thirty minutes per subject — and another few hours over the weekend, you easily hit that target. It is not "too much." It is what you need to be doing.

A guidance counselor at Indian Creek High School in Indiana said, "The number one reason our students don't pass a class is that they fail to turn in their homework. If you take time to figure out the price you pay for skipping a homework assignment, you'll find that in many classes, one missed assignment can drop a grade by half a letter or more."

Keep an assignment book to track your homework. Set a regular time each day for schoolwork. Stay after school in the library to work. Or plan to study from 7:00 to 9:30 every night. There really *is* time for

Lazy?

Lots of students say, "I don't do schoolwork because I'm lazy." But when asked how they spend their time, they say that they are going to school, playing a sport, and working twenty or more hours a week. This doesn't sound like laziness, but it does sound as if they find it easier to work at activities other than school. Certainly, homework is hard when it is mostly about stuff you don't know. If you knew it, you wouldn't need to be in the class. You do boring drills in sports, you tolerate boring tasks at work, you even spend boring time with your friends — and you do it because it makes sense. Try to get your head in a place where doing homework makes sense too.

school, sports, homework, friends, and even a part-time job if you don't waste time. If you are spending more time each week watching TV than doing your homework, you might have one serious conversation with yourself about your priorities.

If you are spending so much time working at a paying job that it is difficult to manage your schoolwork, ask yourself, "Is this the smartest decision for me in the long run?" Chapters 12 and 13 will answer that question.

12. Using School to Start Your Career

Most of us need work to be happy. It takes money to buy what we need and want, and we earn money by working. But when we find work that suits us, we get more than money. We get a sense of worth and satisfaction. **One goal for life after high school is to move toward work that meets your financial and emotional needs.** High school can give you a running start in the direction of both money and satisfaction if you play your cards right.

Schools are beginning to believe that all students — those who are and those who are not considering college — should have both core academic classes *and* career and technology opportunities. But don't count on your high school to figure out how you will take all the right courses and achieve the proper balance — this is a personal decision. Think about what you want and need and design your own program. Be aggressive in asking questions about what is happening throughout your school district. You may be able to find a pilot program that isn't available at your school but suits your interests. Try to plan a high school program that includes both theory and reality, instruction and experience.

Whether or not you decide to apply to college, you should be thinking about additional training after high school. Start asking yourself, "What suits me?" All high schools can offer students ways to begin answering that question. Here is what you should be looking for during your time in high school:

Learn about yourself. What we do well we tend to discount. What we do poorly we tend to magnify. Sometimes it takes a skills inventory — a test that compares how you complete certain tasks compared to others — to appreciate your gifts. For example, you may be gifted in putting things together, remembering musical information, or manipulating numbers. You have an advantage over others when you work from your strengths, so you want to know what they are and figure out where they can best be used.

Career investigation classes help you get an understanding of your skills, interests, and natural temperamental preferences and then help you to match these with career areas in which they can best be put to use. This self-awareness puts you a giant step forward in determining later career choices.

Look into different career possibilities. Once you know what a person in a career you are considering really does, you are in a much better position to make an intelligent decision about your own career.

I interviewed a young man who said he knew he wanted to be a lawyer. His father, grandfather, and great-grandfather had been lawyers, and, of course, he would be one too. However, after he interned at a law firm, he said, "My gosh, all they do is sit. They sit all day and sit all night. I can't stand sitting. I hate being indoors. I don't like detail work."

He quickly gave up the idea of being a lawyer and instead became a talent agent, a career in which he is successful and happy. Without the opportunity to taste and test the life of a lawyer, he might have gone directly to college and law school and only then would he have realized that the life of a lawyer would not make him happy.

Start thinking about career classes in ninth grade. Meet your academic requirements early in your high school career so you'll have time for work-study experiences in your junior and senior years.

Discover your talents. I once met a student in a vocational class on retailing. Rick hadn't asked for the class, but since he wasn't much interested in anything at school, he didn't care where his counselor put him. Class members ran a small school store for other students

continued on next page

and faculty, and to everyone's surprise — including Rick's — Rick had an excellent business sense. He had great marketing ideas, was good at arranging the merchandise, and knew what to buy that would sell well. His success in the store spilled over to other subjects. Suddenly, he discovered math was useful for keeping accounts. And he wanted to learn to write well so he could create advertisements.

Cyrissa discovered the world of emergency medical technicians when she enrolled in a health occupation class. She now works as an EMT on the city ambulances and plans to enter nursing school. Samantha discovered computer graphics in a co-op class her senior year and enrolled in a private technical college to study computer publications. Her boyfriend enjoyed car mechanics but found, instead, he preferred heating and air conditioning as a career — a discovery he might not have made without his high school career training experiences.

Much of career choice is happy accident. A chance encounter with environmental biology issues in a college seminar led an unenthusiastic accounting major to launch a successful career in coastal planning. A co-op job experience, in which you combine work and school training, can evolve from fifteen weeks to a decade, as it did for a young woman who launched her corporate career with Exxon as a high school work-study student. If you're out exploring possibilities and bumping into life, you have more chance of happening on work that suits you.

Accept that it's all right to make mistakes in a safe environment. If you choose career options in high school that you discover are wrong for you, you can pursue other options after high school. If you wait and make these mistakes after high school, you may be paying for your classes and feeling a greater urgency to find your career direction. If you mess up in work-study, you learn from mistakes in a protected situation, have teachers to help you figure out what is going wrong, and avoid having a possible job termination on your work record.

By observing early on the differences between successful and unsuccessful employees, you are more prepared to be effective in

continued on next page

the work world. Whether you are headed to college or not, use high school for career exploration. You may not have the time or the same kinds of opportunities in your college years, and what you learn in career classes may influence your college choice.

Even if you think you are going to be able to prepare yourself to enter the work world at the professional level, you don't want to miss the valuable insights that come from being at ground level. You will be a better supervisor after you have experienced the pressures that face entry-level employees and cope with some of the difficulties, for example, of answering busy phones at an understaffed front desk, working on uncooperative equipment, or receiving orders from many different bosses.

Gain skills that sell in the job market. If you graduate from high school with some skills that employers want or with the preparation that will allow you to enter and complete a specialized training program, you substantially increase your chances of walking into a good job because you will have something of value to offer prospective employers. You can use what you learn in high school to fund your ongoing education with jobs that pay you more than minimum wage because you bring needed skills. But make sure you spend your time learning skills for which there is demand.

Don't tolerate seriously outdated training equipment in high school. You may not need state-of-the-art equipment, but you must be sure that what you are learning must be relevant in the workplace. If you believe your equipment is too outdated for proper instruction, ask your parents to get involved.

Balancing Employment and High School

Many teens need or want paid employment in high school. There are many benefits that come from having paid work experience in your teen years, but there are also some potential problems to consider before you commit to a work schedule.

Schoolwork vs. Job-work Your number one job in high school **is to get an education.** Work outside of school can be an important part of that education but you must find the right balance between schoolwork and paid employment. If working gets in the way of doing homework or getting enough sleep, you need to make some adjustments to your schedule. It may be easier to sell popcorn at the movies or work the cash register at the mall than figure out quadratic equations or subjunctive tenses, but money in your pocket now is not nearly as valuable as education in your head later. Look at the numbers: You are likely to have forty or more years to gain work experience. You are only going to spend four years in high school. Make the most of those four short years.

If you are the kind of person who finds ideas most interesting when you can immediately understand how they apply to and are used in the "real world," you may do better in high school if you also have a job. You can develop a work history as a reliable, trustworthy employee, and this will give you an advantage over other applicants with no work experience. And the money you earn from working may, in fact, make it possible to continue on with your education. But set limits on how much you work, no matter how good the money is. Research suggests that teens who work up to twenty hours per week do better in school than teens who don't work, but teens who work more than twenty hours sharply declined in school performance. This information is compiled from national research on assets that contribute to the developmental well-being of teens. The research was conducted by the Search Institute in Minneapolis in collaboration with the Lutheran Brotherhood. For more information, contact the Search Institute at 700 South Third Street, Minneapolis, MN 55415.

Parent Involvement Be careful, too, about what kinds of deals you negotiate with your parents. In an effort to help you develop a sense of responsibility and fiscal reality, your parents can inadvertently upset your priorities. If you are just getting by in school and your parents say to you, "Yes, you can have a car, but you must save half the money to buy it and make sure you can pay for the gas and insurance," and you agree, you are locking yourself into a certain number of hours of work at a paying job that may make it even harder to focus on schoolwork.

Families have different ways of working these things out. Some families tie material rewards to school performance; others don't. Some expect teenagers to contribute to buying clothes and transportation; others provide an allowance; and still others tie the allowance to household chores. Some families pay money as a reward for good grades and others subtract money for bad ones; some consider only A's and B's acceptable; others are satisfied with C's. Different incentives work in different circumstances. Help your parents figure out what makes sense for you and your family by sitting down and talking with them. Maybe it will help to have some of your friends join in the conversation and discuss how things work in their families. If your parents seem to be standing in the way of your doing what you want, step back for a minute and try to understand their motives.

If you do go job hunting, use all the contacts you have available to you. It is a good feeling to accomplish things on your own, but don't let the natural desire for independence get in the way of letting your parents introduce you to people who can provide experiences in areas that interest you. Smart people at every level make use of the resources they have at hand. Teenagers lucky enough to have parents who can open doors should use the advantage. Getting and keeping the job will be what you do on your own.

How to Find a Career Direction

Each of the following options gives you one more way to use high school to find your career direction.

Take a career investigation course. Some high schools offer career investigation courses that introduce you to many different career groups encompassing hundreds of jobs. Some schools offer a course that allows students to sample careers in one particular career area. You might be able to take an overview of the construction trades or of the health sciences specialties, explore the different career segments of business or of a specific industry like hotels and restaurants. Or your high school might offer a career exploration class that helps you define your interests, skills, and personality preferences in terms of career options.

If you spend time considering lots of different careers early in high school, you will know better what path to follow in your junior and senior year as well as after high school or after college.

Investigate careers independently. If your school doesn't offer career investigation courses or you don't have room in your schedule to take advantage of the opportunity, organize a do-it-yourself program. It's likely that your school has a computer career planning program in the library, counselors' office, or career office such as CHOICES, COIN, DISCOVER, or EXPAN. Schedule a time to go through the program independently and then talk about the results with your counselor, parents, or mentor. Many public libraries also provide computers with career assessment programs and career information. Call your library to see what they offer.

An excellent source of career information is the Armed Services

Vocational Aptitude Battery, ASVAB. The military gives this two-and-a-half-hour comprehensive test to help recruit students for the armed forces. You can take the test even if you are not interested in the military. Results for each student are prepared individually and sent to your counselor. They include helpful information regarding your aptitudes as compared to other students'. If the ASVAB isn't scheduled at your school, talk with your counselor about inviting a recruiter to administer it.

The easiest — and I think least used — way to find out about careers is to talk with people who live them. Students can get general information on any career by looking in the book *Dictionary of Occupations*. You can find it in the library or on-line via the National School to Work Learning and Information Center. Their "answer line" number is 1-800-251-7236; the Internet address is http://www.stw.ed.gov. Many states also have State Occupational Information Coordinating Committees (SOICC) that give students useful career information, which may include printouts on careers of interest to you. A printed sheet describing any career is, by itself, pretty dry. It comes alive only when you talk with people in those careers of interest.

Family members or friends may know people who are doing work in your areas of interest. Ask for their help in introducing you. It has always seemed easier to me to call someone who knows I am calling than to call cold, but if you have to call without an introduction, take the plunge and do it.

Enroll in a magnet or career and technology program. Most high school districts offer a series of courses that prepare students for the work world and/or teach job-specific skills. But some high schools, usually in larger school districts, have a special career focus, for example, engineering, fine arts, computers, or health sciences. The best time to think about getting into these classes is while choosing a high school for ninth grade. If you are interested in an area that is not offered at your zoned school, you may be eligible to transfer to a school that offers classes in your areas of interest.

Think smart! If you have a choice, pick a school based on the education it can give you, not on where your current friends are headed.

More and more schools are developing a new blend of academics and career training called Tech Prep, which is based on the belief that vocational training should start early and continue for at least two years of post–high school training. Tech Prep programs have carefully designed "course sequences" that can take a student from high school to college to graduate school. You acquire very specific and useful job skills along the way, and you can get on or off the academic track or move completely onto the work track at any point after high school.

See the information in Chapter 14, Different Ways to Do High School.

Use the summer to explore opportunities. Use your summers to gain work experience. Paying jobs are great, but if you can't find one that helps you learn what you are looking for, consider other options:

- Locate the right volunteer opportunity. Do a good job volunteering and you will walk away with skills and references to help you land a paid job.

- Find a person who knows what it is you want to learn. Ask if they will take you on as an apprentice, and in return for your free work, agree to spend a specified amount of time each week teaching you their skills.

- Look for short courses in your community that teach specific skills. Many big cities offer Leisure Learning classes. Others have community education programs connected to the public school district, the community college, or private colleges and universities. You can, for example, spend a few weeks learning such diverse skills as how to tune your car, use a computer software application, decorate a cake professionally, or design a newsletter.

- Teach yourself. Lots of teens get good at things like installing software, designing clothes, or fixing electronic equipment by treating these skills as hobbies. Spending time on things you enjoy is a pleasure, but if you become an expert in your area, your pleasure can also become your work.

Look for a mentor. Sometimes, we can listen to adults who are not our parents more easily than we can listen to our parents. Many students benefit from having a career mentor — a person who is involved in and concerned with your successes — as another caring adult in their lives.

Career and technology teachers may be able to help you connect with a mentor. Ask your counselor if your school has a mentoring program. If you think you need a mentor and can't find one through school, try writing a letter to the director of human resources at a company that employs people in your area of interest. Explain that you are interested in a career mentor and ask if they would be able to connect you with an interested employee. Let your parents know what you are doing and make sure they meet the mentor if he or she doesn't come through an organized school program.

What if you are approaching the end of high school and nothing seems interesting? Try this. Decide what kind of lifestyle you think you would like to live. Sit down with your parents or other adults and figure out how much you will have to earn in a year to live the way you want. Want a nice house in a good neighborhood? What will it cost? How much will you pay for the car you want to drive? How about insurance, taxes, maintenance, and improvements to your property? Figure your lifestyle choices, such as eating in restaurants, going to movies, buying expensive shoes, taking vacations, giving people gifts, paying for dry cleaning, and contributing to charity, into your budget. Then develop the amount you think you need to earn each year to maintain this lifestyle. Then add 10 percent for emergencies and things you forgot. Remember to subtract health insurance premiums and taxes from the dollars you decide you want to be paid. Now, what kinds of jobs can you prepare for that will give you the life you are describing? Which jobs use your preferred kind of intelligence? Chapter 10 provides further information on this subject.

Choosing the Best Career and Technology Experiences

Do *not* make school decisions based on hearsay. If you are in a large district that has high schools with different programs, go in person to check out the programs not offered at your zoned school.

Unfortunately, there isn't always an easy way to find out which career and technology programs will be best for you. The quality of programs from one district to another and even one school to another can vary. Most school systems are not able to provide information about the quality of training or the success of students in using their training to find jobs. The only way to find out what's good, what's right for you, and where there is space, is to go looking. Ask counselors, teachers, graduates, employers, and friends. Visit with current and former students. *Do whatever it takes to get to the right place* because this is your time and your career. Do it right and it can also be your fatter paycheck.

Managing your Choices It can be difficult to get into popular career classes or transfer to a school for career reasons in the middle of high school. Most schools have clearly specified processes for transferring. Find out what the rules are; get any forms you need to complete to transfer; fill them out early and return them, but make a copy for yourself first and another copy to give to your current counselor. It also wouldn't hurt to send a copy directly to the teacher who is in charge of the program you want to enter.

If you know a program is right for you, don't just fill in a form and leave it for your counselor. Go to the school or program you want to attend and have a conference with the appropriate teacher about getting admitted. Ask to talk to other students. *Let the teacher know you are really serious about this class, that you are determined to take it.* Find out if the principal at the school to which you want to transfer must sign the transfer form. If so, take it with you when you visit. If you convey enthusiasm, make the effort to look over the work area and get to know the person who is teaching, you have a better chance of winning a class spot when programs are too crowded to take all applicants.

If you don't get your transfer form back with a response in the time period you are told to expect, follow up with a phone call. If your transfer is rejected, usually there is an appeals process. The earlier in your high school career that you transfer to a career program, the more training you will get. Allow enough time for backup choices. If you cannot get into a program at one school, repeat the process for another. In the meantime, start investigating the options for training in your preferred area after high school. If your parents can help you manage the transfer and career exploration process, let them get involved.

How to Make Sure You Get a Chance at the Classes That Introduce You to Employment Opportunities It used to be that if you couldn't compete in your academic classes, well, you could slide into vocational education. Some people still think career and technology classes are where you find unsuccessful students. *Wrong! Wrong by a mile!*

Good vocational programs teach more than one skill. They provide you with a solid academic base that includes abstract and conceptual thinking as well as technical expertise and its applications. These programs usually have many more applicants than spaces.

If you haven't established a record of reliability, you will have a hard time getting into the good classes. Ellen McGonigle, who teaches office education classes at Milby High School in Houston, explains that students are not accepted into her Business Co-op class unless they pass the state-mandated achievement test (TAAS), have all the required academic credits in good order, have decent grades, and have a good attendance record. She states:

> If you have to take remedial work for the TAAS test or you have to make up classes you failed, you don't have time in your schedule to work. And if you don't have decent grades and good attendance, the companies we work with, like Tenneco and Lyondell, don't want

you. . . . But if you get into our classes, you can get wonderful work experience, earn money for college, and, often, go from high school co-op to college co-op with the same company.

While all career and technology classes don't set such high standards, heavy competition for popular classes means teachers can select students they think will make good use of the opportunity. With more students now competing for these classes, many classes have more students who want in than spaces for them.

If you are unable to get a specific class that you want, don't despair. Though high school will help you become familiar with specific career areas, it is meant primarily to develop your general skills. You want to build a solid academic foundation and gain a general understanding of what makes people employable. After you graduate, you can choose a training program that concentrates on specific vocational skills.

Here's the deal: as we move to the twenty-first century, dumb is out. Being cool by hanging out and cutting school is only for the no-bodys. You learned to walk, climb, and jump when it was time. You learned to talk and read. Now it's time to comprehend and compute at a higher level, to think abstractly and develop problem-solving skills, to develop discipline and judgment.

Looking Ahead to Working After You Graduate

What's a Career and What's a Job? A career is your life's work. Satisfying careers often are marked by a progression of jobs within an occupational area. An example of a career unfolding is a progression from waiter to trainer to head waiter to assistant director of a catering company, assistant manager of a hotel food service department, and then general manager of a successful restaurant. A job is one stop in the area — being a fingerprint clerk in the area of law enforcement, a lab tech in the area of health care or a sales person in the area of sales and marketing, for example. A little luck helps but preparation and hard work help more. When you find yourself with increasingly demanding jobs, increasingly better skills, more personal satisfaction, and higher pay, you know you have gone beyond working a job to building your career.

Supply and Demand Every job requires specific skills. If a job only requires basic skills that many people can bring to it, it will pay less. If it needs more complicated skills that fewer people have, it will usually pay you more. Star athletes are paid a great deal of money because very few people can do what they do, and many people are interested in paying to watch them do it. Taking care of little children or fixing engines is just as important — or more important — than winning a championship game. However, more people have child care or mechanical skills and fewer people are willing to pay dearly for these skills, so these jobs pay less than professional basketball.

This is the concept of supply and demand, and it affects how much money you will make. If demand (the number of people who want a product or service) is large and supply (the amount that is out there for people to buy) is small — diamonds, for example — the price goes up. If the supply is large and the demand is small (used tires, for example), the price for the product goes way down. If you develop skills that employers want but not enough people have, you will earn more for your work and have more job opportunities. Skills you develop in high school can complement the basket of skills you develop in college or post–secondary education and make you more valuable when it is time to enter the job market. According to Kenneth B. Hoyt at Kansas State University, during the years 1994 through 2005, the *annual* number of college graduates who are job seekers (1,340,000) is expected to exceed the number of expected job openings requiring a college degree (1,040,000). Since there will be about 300,000 more college graduates than jobs requiring a college degree for the next five to ten years, the more experiences you have, the better your chances in the employment market.

What if you are now a sophomore or a junior and didn't get started on a college or career plan in ninth grade? Jump in! Find out the sequence of courses for a career area that interests you. Make a chart that lists all of these courses. Fill in the ones you have already taken. Figure out how you can fit in everything else. Include enough classes to give you the option of doing college work, too. You may want to go to summer school, spend an extra semester in school, or take beginning career courses at a community college. And if you find at the end of high school that your choice doesn't suit you anymore, you can switch to something else with a good deal of self-knowledge.

If you are a senior and you have been drifting with no clear direction and now graduation is drawing closer, you need to get a plan fast. Chapter 17 will help you sort through your next steps.

13. Getting Real About the World of Work

How Does Your Education Affect How Much Money You Can Earn?

When a group of high school students reviewed the material in this book, one student said: "You know, if they paid us to go to school, we would do much better. Why don't they pay us to come here?"

Students do get paid to go to school! You just don't get the money right away.

- Most of us will work for forty years or more. Full-time workers will spend 2,080 hours a year in their jobs — 83,200 work hours over forty years. According to Labor Department statistics, people with a college degree are, on average, likely to earn $6.75 an hour more than people with jobs that require no more than three months training. That means that in forty years, you are likely to earn $479,232 more because of your college education.

- In the thirty-five highest paying occupations, full-time workers in these jobs earn, on average, about $22.18 per hour, or $46,134 per year. People in the thirty-five lowest paying occupations, on average, earn $4.96 per hour, or $10,275 per year. (This will adjust upward slightly with increases in the minimum wage, but the increases will do little to reduce the huge pay scale gap.) In general, people in the highest paying occupations have more education and people in the lowest paying occupations have little or poor education.

- Wages have fallen for 75 percent of the population without college degrees in recent decades. In 1979, the average hourly wage of a high school graduate was $11.23. For a college graduate, it was $15.52. By 1993, the college graduates' wages had only risen to $15.71 but the high school graduates' wages had fallen to $9.93 — a 58 percent penalty for less education.

How Education Affects Wages

The median annual earnings of year-round full-time workers is directly impacted by education level:

Education Level	Mean Annual Earnings
Professional	$74,560
Doctorate	$54,904
Master's degree	$40,368
Bachelor's degree	$32,629
Associate degree	$24,398
Some college, no degree	$19,666
High school diploma	$18,737
Not a high school graduate	$12,809

This data is taken from the summer 1992 *Occupational Outlook Quarterly* by K. J. Shelley as reported by the Counseling for High Skills Project at Kansas State University and from the winter 1994–95 *Occupational Outlook Quarterly* article by T. Cosca, pages 38–46, also reported in KSU Counseling for High Skills materials. Different sources report slightly different numbers; however, the sense of the numbers does not change.

Formal higher education is not the only avenue to increased income. Skills are important factors in employment and income. One out of every six full-time salaried work force participants aged twenty-five or older (more than 9 million workers) who did not have a four-year college degree earned $700 or more each week. That is not much different from the median earnings for college graduates. Of workers under age 35 without college degrees, one in twenty earns $1,000 or more a week. Skills can compensate for the absence of formal education.

What does this mean for you as a high school student today? You could be the rare high school dropout who earns a million dollars — but the chances of that happening are as unlikely as winning the lottery. The message is, *Learning is earning. The more education you have, the more money you are likely to make and the less likely you are to be unemployed.*

So, to the guy who wants to be paid to go to high school, let him consider that not only will he get the financial payoff of education over the forty years to come, but in high school, he gets this education free. After that, in community colleges, universities, technical schools, or trade schools, he pays!

Is College Essential?

The U.S. Department of Labor predicts that between 1992 and 2010, only about twenty-three percent of the newly created jobs in the United States will require a college degree. However, 75 percent of future jobs are likely to want employees to have at least a license or certificate. An ever-increasing number of employers will be looking for employees with higher-level skills — particularly math, language, and reasoning skills — even when a college degree is not required. You can develop many marketable skills in high school if you take school seriously and work at it. It is wise, however, in this labor market, to recognize that most of your specific work skills will come after high school.

While college graduates on average earn more, a college degree does not guarantee a good job or a high income. Nearly a quarter of all college graduates in the coming years are likely to find themselves, at least in their initial jobs, working in positions that do not require a college education. Yet college helps students develop the general skills that ultimately give them more flexibility and options in the work world.

People who combine the skills of creative thinking, decision making, problem solving, and conceptualizing are on the road to success.

It is not necessary to attend college to develop these skills, and not all college graduates have acquired them. What is most important is *what you know*, not where you learned it, and *how you perform* in the workplace.

The more skills you have, the more valuable you are in the workplace. Suppose you can fix things easily. That's an advantage. But if you can write memos and reports as well, you'll be even more valuable. Add to that, for example, computer skills, and you would be an especially valuable employee because you could move easily from one assignment to another. In short: *learn lots!* And learn it well. There is always room in the work force for someone who is outstanding.

"Nothing turns out to be irrelevant," advises an experienced career counselor. Whatever you are doing, where you are working, and what you are learning usually turns out to have value down the line. The more you learn, the more people you meet, and the more experiences you have, the more likely that you will stand out from the crowd and be the person who gets the job.

Yes, There Are Jobs Every day, people get hired. Every day employers always look for people who can meet their particular needs. The challenge is to figure out where the jobs are and to present yourself to employers in a winning way. You can find jobs advertised in the newspaper, posted on bulletin boards, through contacts with friends and relatives, through unions and professional associations, through private and public employment agencies and, increasingly, through the Internet. Internet sites help you scan job openings. A good place to begin is Best Bets from the Net, a University of Michigan service that categorizes and reviews various career sites. Their Internet address is http://www.lib.umich.edu/chdocs/employment/.

In the early nineties, a group called TechForce 2000 studied eight jobs at Houston's Texas Medical Center that could be filled by people with only a high school diploma and on-the-job training. TechForce 2000 found that more than 50 percent of the people who applied were judged unprepared to handle even entry-level jobs. Of those who were hired for these jobs, with starting pay from $12,506 to $22,621 a year plus full benefits and the possibility of merit increases, about half resigned or were terminated within one year. Many were fired because they did not know how to behave in a work situation or could not meet employer expectations.

There are jobs for high school graduates with little or no additional training. In fact, 10 million jobs in the next decade are projected for people with only high school educations. But too many young men and women will not get or keep these jobs because they did not learn what they need to know in high school. Those who will have the best chance of advancing from lower-paying entry level jobs to better-paying promotions will have acquired additional training. Labor market statistics show clearly that the greatest number of job openings will be for employees with some form of post-secondary education less than a bachelor's degree.

Where Are the Job Opportunities? To learn about job openings in your state, get in touch with your State Occupational Information Coordinating Committee (SOICC). There are SOICCs in every state, and their mandate is to provide occupational information to all who seek it. Services differ from state to state, but every state is developing databases about future job needs for that state, and all SOICCs should be able to refer you to the right place for school-to-work information if they cannot help you directly.

As you look at your choices, think about the difference between a job and a career. You may want to begin after high school with a job that helps you become comfortable in the world of work, and then focus on how to gain additional skills that can help you shape a career with opportunity for advancement. A salary that is acceptable to you at nineteen may not comfortably support a family and allow you to save for retirement in later years.

State Occupational Information Coordinating Councils

Alabama	(334) 242-2990	Missouri	(573) 751-3800
Alaska	(907) 465-4518	Montana	(406) 444-2741
American Samoa	(684) 633-4485	Nebraska	(402) 471-9953
Arizona	(602) 542-3871	Nevada	(702) 687-4550
Arkansas	(501) 682-3159	New Hampshire	(603) 228-3349
California	(916) 323-6544	New Jersey	(609) 292-2682
Colorado	(303) 620-4981	New Mexico	(505) 841-8455
Connecticut	(203) 638-4042	New York	(518) 457-3806
Delaware	(302) 761-8050	North Carolina	(919) 733-6700
District of		North Dakota	(701) 328-9734
Columbia	(202) 724-7237	Ohio	(614) 466-1109
Florida	(904) 488-1048	Oklahoma	(405) 743-5198
Georgia	(404) 656-9639	Oregon	(503) 378-5747
Guam	(671) 649-9759	Pennsylvania	(717) 772-2168
Hawaii	(808) 586-8750	Puerto Rico	(787) 723-7110
Idaho	(208) 334-3705	Rhode Island	(401) 272-0830
Illinois	(217) 785-0789	South Carolina	(803) 737-2733
Indiana	(317) 233-5099	South Dakota	(605) 626-2314
Iowa	(515) 242-4889	Tennessee	(615) 741-6451
Kansas	(913) 296-2387	Texas	(512) 502-3750
Kentucky	(502) 564-4258	Utah	(801) 536-7806
Louisiana	(504) 342-5149	Vermont	(802) 229-0311
Maine	(207) 624-6200	Virgin Islands	(809) 776-3700
Maryland	(410) 767-2953		x2036
Massachusetts	(617) 626-5718	Washington	(360) 438-4803
Michigan	(517) 373-0363	West Virginia	(304) 759-0724
Minnesota	(612) 296-2072	Wisconsin	(608) 267-9611
Mississippi	(601) 949-2240	Wyoming	(307) 473-3809

The Dictionary of Occupational Titles is an encyclopedia of careers covering hundreds of occupations and dozens of industries. (*The Occupational Outlook Handbook* lists ALL occupations.) You can find these books in the library and on-line through the National School-to-Work Learning and Information Center (see below). Use written materials to stimulate your thinking about career choices, learn about careers that are unfamiliar to you and find out just what various jobs require and reward.

What Happens If You Drop Out of High School? What happens to school dropouts? *Not much.* According to a U.S. Bureau of Labor study, high school dropouts have only four chances in ten of finding employment during their first year out of school. Eventually, six out of ten dropouts find some kind of job, but four of the ten will remain unemployed. Compare this to high school graduates: more than eight of ten find jobs. If you are determined to drop out, talk with your counselor about moving directly into a job training program.

Having Vision Means More Than Eyesight High school graduates in the work force are likely to change jobs nine times and occupations as much as seven or more times in their lifetime. If you are in high school today, you can expect even more changes in your lifetime. Those who take one day at a time and believe the future will take care of itself are less likely to do well in this work world than those who look ahead and ask, "Where do I want to go and what do I need to get there?" People who do best in a changing world have vision — that is, they form a picture of where they want to go and figure out how to get there. People most likely to lose out are those who don't look ahead, who don't prepare and don't keep growing and learning.

Why People Lose Their Jobs In the Prior Report (from information distributed by the Texas State Occupational Information Coordinating Committee), employers listed the seven behaviors most likely to cost you your job:

Why People Get Their Jobs

Employers won't hire you because you "want a job." Lots of people want jobs — but don't want to work very hard. Employers hire you not because of what *you* want but because they believe you might provide what *they* want. In general, employers want employees who

- are judged to be honest;
- seem intelligent enough to do the work well;
- are willing and able to learn new things;
- appear reliable and responsible;
- have some previous experience doing this kind of work or related work;
- have people known to the employer vouch for their character and/or ability;
- offer good references from previous work experiences;
- appear eager and interested and willing to try hard.

1. Dishonesty
2. Irresponsibility/goofing off
3. Arrogance/ego problems
4. Absenteeism/lateness
5. Inability to follow directions or company policy
6. Whining and complaining
7. Laziness and lack of commitment

People also lose their jobs because of the downsizing that occurs when new machines replace people or companies figure out how to do their work with fewer employees. Many big businesses are now in the process of downsizing. It is often the small and medium-sized companies that are growing; more than 10 percent of all jobs are now in small firms,

How to Find Help When You're Job Hunting

Are you one of the many teens who wish you could have more career counseling and better job-hunting advice? There is, happily, more printed information and more places to call than there has ever been.

All kinds of printed information about how to fill out applications, prepare your résumé, write job hunting letters and handle yourself in a job interview is out there waiting for you to read it. There are pages of ideas about where to look for job openings and excellent advice about how to get started. Look for these resources in your counselor's office. Look in the library or bookstore, visit the career and placement office of your closest college and ask the SOICC staff. Take advantage of the reams of helpful advice that you can use for free.

Call the person who heads your school district's career and technology (or vocational education) program and ask what kinds of resources your district has. Often there are career fairs, career seminars and job-hunting classes if you go looking for them. If you cannot track down what you need, call the National School-to-Work Learning and Information Center in Washington, D.C., at 1-800-251-7236. This center is building a resource database for parents and students, teachers, trainers, and employers. They will help you find out where to go for the information you need. (400 Virginia Ave. SW, Room 210, Washington, D.C. 20024. Fax: (202) 401-6211; e-mail: stw-lc@ed.gov.)

If you have access to the Internet, there are a growing number of sites with career information. Try CareerWeb, http://www.cweb.com, as a starting point.

---

and the percentage is likely to grow. Small companies without many employees especially value staff members who are flexible, quick to learn, adaptable and reliable. These companies need workers who can think about the health and welfare of the business like bosses. Young workers who understand the opportunities this kind of thinking provides can expect to do well.

Pay now or pay later. Those who work at getting an education in high school are likely to be rewarded for their efforts with more money and better jobs. There are jobs to be had, thousands of them, and there is no reason why a good job cannot be yours — but it will not come to you. You must prepare to find it.

14. Different Ways to Do High School

I took some high school students out to lunch recently. One ordered pizza with pepperoni. One ordered a hamburger and fries; and one was a vegetarian who ordered a salad. Everyone was happy. Just as pizza is not the same as hamburgers, one high school is not the same as another.

You will spend four years in high school. That's 36 months — or 144 weeks — more than 4,800 hours. If your district offers you choices, why not spend all that time in a place that suits you and helps you do your best?

Many students have only one high school they can attend, but students in big city districts can find a whole menu of possibilities. Lots of students with a choice pick a school because that's where their friends are going. *Big* mistake. Don't do this! If you choose to go to a different high school than your eighth grade friends are attending, you will, in short order, make new friends. Even if you go where everybody else is going, you are likely to have different friends in twelfth grade than you had in eighth grade.

How Does a Middle School Student Choose Which High School to Attend?

It would be so convenient if we could fast forward from middle school to middle age, take a quick polaroid of the world and the way we feel about it, then come back and plan our high school education with the future in mind. Unfortunately, the best we can do is imagine what we will want and need in the years ahead.

If you are thirteen or fourteen, it's natural to be more concerned with what will happen tonight and tomorrow, with your friends and your personal life, than with a distant future. I know it is hard to ask you to imagine how you might see the world when you are in your twenties or thirties — but this is the time when you make important decisions about high school, and without looking ahead, you can't make the best decision.

The general rule for high school placement in most school districts is that you go to the school that serves your neighborhood, often called your zoned school, unless you have been accepted into another school for a special program or as a transfer. When you have high school choices, the easiest time to transfer into a school outside your neighborhood is at the beginning of ninth grade.

Many ninth graders reported that they made their school decision based on poor information. They decide they don't like something without ever really finding out about it. They decide they won't get in, so they don't bother to apply. They decide it's too "difficult" to decide, so they don't do anything. Or they read a description that sounds good, and, without finding out any more information, decide, *"That's for me."* Don't do this!

I asked Nina Strattner, the executive assistant to the New York City Superintendent of High Schools, what she would be sure to include if she were writing this book, and she shot right back, "I wish all kids would visit the high school they think they want to attend before they get there. We spend an enormous amount of time with children who make the wrong choice." You may not be able to visit all your choices, but you and a parent can and should visit the schools that most interest you.

Check out the commute, check out the classes, check out the general feel of the school before deciding it is the right place for you. Don't overlook a sixty-minute commute because of a friend or the lure of a special class without considering that two hours a day spent on travel will limit many other activities. Don't wait until you are enrolled and classes are under way to get the feel of a school, for in many cities you cannot transfer until you have completed a semester — and then you can only choose schools that have available space. Let your parents help you with this important decision. They may not be perfectly tuned in to what you are thinking, but they bring ideas and experiences that you haven't had yet. If you work together with your parents on this, you are likely to make a better choice than if you ignore them.

If most students in your high school continue on to post–high school education, the odds tilt toward your continuing your education. If most students score below average on standardized tests, you increase your odds of also scoring below average. If the majority of students are interested in science, you are likely to learn lots about science, too. Do yourself the favor of surrounding yourself with people who create success. It's easier to go with the odds than against them. Teens are better off in a high school where most ninth graders graduate four years later and pass required tests. If your public high school has a bad track record, you are going to have to be extra attentive to make sure you don't get caught in a syndrome of low achievement. Look for programs within the high school that fight the odds — Upward Bound, honors, leadership teams, ROTC — whatever program is working is where you want to be — or look for ways to get yourself into a school where success is in the air.

Making Changes

When Things Aren't Working Out Most everybody starts high school with at least a few nervous thoughts, but after a few months, you begin to feel you'll be O.K. If, however, school is not going well — and this means failing classes, showing a poor attitude, feeling depressed, feeling bored, having no friends — it's time to take a hard look at what's going on and figure out a way to change things. If your parents and your counselor do not understand that you are having trouble, then you take the lead, call them all together and ask for their support and their advice. Do *not*, do *not*, do *not* let yourself continue in a situation that is bringing you failure, depression, boredom or danger.

All sorts of things quite normally knock teenagers out of balance. It is not unusual for academically gifted students to do poorly from lack of challenge or fear of teasing or for students struggling with learning problems to act out to divert attention from the real problem. Problems at home — divorce, sickness, money worries, fighting — can make you feel crazy. Misguided friends can introduce liquor or drugs into your life, and you may get caught up in damaging conformity that leads you to behave in a way that isn't really you. Next thing you know your school performance is slipping, and so is your self-esteem.

Do you know that you're hanging out with the wrong people, but you don't want to walk away? The solution: get so busy doing something else that you have a good excuse to be elsewhere. Get involved in work-study; volunteer; throw yourself into working on the stage crew for the school musical; start training for biking, hiking, rowing or running. Do you know you are messing up academically but don't want to deal with it? Is this because you don't think you will like doing what it takes to succeed? O.K., you really need to open up with adults in your life who can support you in making changes. If you will take some risks and be open to change, you may be surprised at what unfolds. The solution is not to have someone *make* you do what you don't want to do. It is to help you get to a place where you *want* to do what you need to do on your own. You don't have to know the answer, but you have to start searching for what it might be.

Nonnie, a seventeen-year-old with a history of school failure, found success for the first time when she joined the Seaborne Conservation Corps, a ship-based residential GED program run in conjunction with the U.S. Navy and Texas A&M University. And Tony, who decided it was too risky to appear smart in his local high school, felt he could be his "real self" only when he went to boarding school. "I didn't realize I was unhappy," he said, "until I found out what it felt like to be really contented."

Take control. Remember, this is *your* life, and it can be a good and happy life if you decide that you deserve just that and set out to find it. But failure won't get you there, and neither will depression, boredom, drugs, or alcohol. You may be able to turn an unsatisfactory situation around right in your own school, or you may have to switch to a school that is better suited to you. Do whatever you must to make high school *work* for *you* because you need this foundation on which to build your future.

Finding the Right School Some years ago in St. Louis, I was the executive director of an association of pre-collegiate private schools. Parents would call and ask, "Will you tell me which is the best school?"

"Yes," I'd answer, "but best for whom? First you have to tell me about your child and about you and then I can tell you which is best."

Some teens do best in highly structured environments, and others do terribly. Some teens benefit greatly from small classes and close attention; others thrive in chaotic, crowded high schools. Kinesthetic kids need to move and be involved in sports. Artistic kids deserve the chance to use their gifts. Sensitive kids need schools where they aren't constantly judged, and highly social teens with average academic skills need schools that don't overvalue grades and tests. You can't always have exactly what you need, but if you don't think about what works well for you and look for it, you certainly won't find it.

When you and your parents visit a school, either public or private, begin the conversation by asking, "What kinds of students are most likely to do well here and what kinds of students seem to do less well in this environment?" If the answer is, "We have all kinds of students and they all do fine," push harder to get more information. Ask what the school thinks it does well and what it wants to improve. A school that doesn't have anything it wants to improve is a school to be wary of.

Before you consider private schools, find out about *all* the public high school choices in your district. A tuition-free program that is right for you may exist without your knowing about it. In cities, there are many options for students, including magnet schools, vocational and technology schools, special schools, and honors schools. If you live in a small town with no school choice, perhaps it is possible to take a year abroad by living with family members in another city so you can experience a different school setting. If you consider this, make sure the new school district will accept you under these circumstances and find out if there is tuition to be paid.

Magnet School Considerations

1. Magnet schools give teens a *focus*, which helps some students do well. Magnet school students often develop a group spirit because their numbers are small — the student body is smaller.
2. Magnet classes are often smaller than regular school classes, and magnet students are more likely to be given individual attention. Many programs select for ability and have a college-bound, achievement-oriented environment.
3. Magnet programs, especially those that emphasize academics, may give more homework and are often more demanding than typical high school programs. You will be expected to do the work or leave the program.
4. Magnet students come from all over the city, so it may be difficult to find friends who live near you. You can counter this by playing in local sports leagues, joining youth groups that serve your neighborhood, and finding an extracurricular connection to your zoned school (though the school social dynamics are different).
5. Magnet programs are organized in different ways. Some magnet schools are schoolwide and all students in the school are part of the magnet program. Classes may be smaller and there may be great enrichment in the magnet area, but there may be less choice in other electives and in high-level academic courses. In magnet schools that are not located within regular high schools, there are often no organized athletics. To participate in school sports, band or orchestra, cheerleading and drill team, students must return to their zoned school after classes. This can be a transportation problem and sometimes a social problem.

   Some magnet programs are self-contained in a regular high school. That means that students can participate in sports and extracurriculars within the school but that all academic classes are with other magnet students.

continued on next page

In certain magnet programs, students are part of the regular school and they come together only for classes in the magnet subject area. Students take honors or regular classes that are offered by the general high school. In these cases it is important to get a sense of the whole high school program as well as the magnet program.

6. Some magnet programs are housed in schools that are predominantly one race. Sometimes, parents from other ethnic groups won't consider a magnet program because of this. In researching this book, I looked for magnet students who were not part of the majority racial group and asked them what they thought I should write. Maybe those who were unhappy didn't voice their opinions, but I didn't find a single student who advised me to make race an issue in choosing a magnet program. What they did say was, "You have to know who you are and not bring prejudices with you . . . If you are easy about people, it's no big deal." One student added an interesting insight: "Being a minority has been as important for my education as anything I learned in class. Sometimes it felt a little weird, but I am really glad I did this."

7. If a magnet program does not suit you, you can transfer back to your zoned school unless your school is overcrowded and in danger of being closed for enrollment. Check with your zoned school to make sure there is space before withdrawing from a magnet program.

Magnet School Programs

Magnet school programs provide a high school education that is organized around a special subject area, like performing arts or health sciences. In some cities, the magnet schools are perceived to provide a more attractive learning environment than many zoned high schools.

The kinds of choices offered and the rules and regulations for magnet schools will vary from city to city. You must, of course, find out exactly what is offered in your community. This information is generic and while it will be useful in most situations, yours may be different. Check with your district for local specifics.

Admission to Magnet Schools If you live in a district with several magnet school choices, the district is likely to have very specific policies about how students apply. Usually it is all written down, and you will want to get a copy of this explanation. If the school district holds meetings for parents, go and listen to the explanation as well.

Call the district headquarters and ask if there is a magnet school office or coordinator. Find out when meetings occur, when applications are due, if there is a standard application form or if each magnet school has its own form and what the school visiting arrangements are for parents and potential students. Ask if you can apply to as many magnet programs as you wish. Take advantage of this option if you have it.

Transferring After Ninth Grade Four-year magnet schools take the majority of students in the ninth grade. Most programs, however, accept a few tenth graders. Fewer students, if any, are admitted in eleventh grade. If you aren't accepted into a program that you believe is right for you in the ninth grade, make an appointment with the magnet coordinator in April or May, when the admissions work is over, and explain that you will reapply in tenth grade. Ask the magnet coordinator which courses you should take and which requirements you must meet in order to be in a good position to apply the next year. Let the coordinator see that you are really serious about this program. Then do what you say you are going to do and apply again, enclosing a note reminding the coordinator of your earlier discussion.

Private Schools

Sometimes it happens that your zoned school is not a good fit for you. Perhaps you can improve the fit by making schedule changes or making adjustments within yourself. If you and your family, however, wish to consider private schools, begin by talking about what kind of school is going to help you do your best before you start naming specific schools. Private schools can focus on special concerns and particular approaches to learning in smaller settings. But just because a school is private doesn't mean it is necessarily better. Private schools, like public schools, have strengths and weaknesses.

A school is "best" for you if it fits your needs, your learning style, your social values, your financial circumstances, and your personality. Just because someone tells you a school is terrific does not mean it will be terrific for you. Visit the schools you are considering and talk with students who attend them now.

Tuition at private schools varies. At the low end, it can be around $3,500 a year. At the high end, it can approach $12,000 — even more if you choose a boarding school. Many private schools offer partial scholarships based on need. Do not hesitate to sit down with the admissions director or financial aid officer to discuss your financial concerns and the options for funding tuition.

Military, religious, special education, and nonsectarian private schools all fall in the private school category. They are listed in subsections under the heading of Schools in the yellow pages. Most of those with high school programs have small or large advertisements that tell you they serve teens. *Peterson's Guide to Private Secondary Schools* lists 1,400 accredited schools worldwide. You can get a directory of boarding schools by calling the Association of Boarding Schools, 1-800-541-5908. Look at the information in the front of *Peterson's* for a general overview of how to evaluate private schools and how schools admit students. (You will find that Peterson's Guides are recommended several times in this book. They offer many different kinds of books to meet most student needs; they are comprehensive and current; and they are available in most bookstores in most parts of the country. There are, however, many good books on the market. I encourage you to find the ones that are most appealing to you.)

In many cities, there are trained consultants who can help families sort through private school decisions. If you are looking for a consultant in your area, you can contact the Independent Educational Consultants Association, P.O. Box 125, Forrestdale, MA 02644-0125; (508) 833-0670. There are a few unusual schools that are organized specifically for young people who cannot afford private school tuition but would benefit from a residential school program. One is the Eagle Rock School in Estes Park, Colorado. Founded by the Honda Corporation, Eagle Rock is a year-round, residential high school for one hundred students who are not finding success in their current schools but are willing and ready to change, learn, and cooperate. For information, call (970) 586-0600 or write P.O. Box 1770, Estes Park, CO 80517-1770. Another is the Milton Hershey School in Hershey, Pennsylvania, a K–12 coed boarding school for children from disadvantaged families. Students must enroll at this school by age sixteen, and most receive complete scholarships. For more information, write P.O. Box 2000, Paoli, PA 19301, or call (610) 363-5346. Counselors at your high school may also know of private schools in your area designed to address your needs.

If it is unsafe for you to continue living at home, this does *not* mean you must drop out of school to earn money for your own apartment. Get in touch with the United Way in your community or in a big city near you and ask for help in finding a safe place to live while you complete your high school education. There are some schools around the country especially for young people whose home life is unsafe physically or emotionally. You will be able to live with other teens and go to school free of worry.

15. Special Education

In Chapter 10, I confessed that I am a terrible musician. If schools valued musical ability as much as reading and writing abilities, I could not function without special help. I would still be the same capable person I am now, but I would not be capable of meeting demands for musical achievement. If school requires you to do things that you cannot do without help, then you'll want to find assistance.

Special education sometimes gets a bad rap because we forget that we all have abilities and disabilities. In school, the disabilities that qualify you for special education services are:

- learning disabilities
- physical handicaps
- mental handicaps
- emotional handicaps
- autism
- speech impairments
- traumatic brain injury
- visual handicaps
- hearing impairment
- other health impairment

Attention deficit disorder, although a prevalent learning problem, is not a category of its own, but services can be provided under other categories such as "other health impaired" and "emotional disturbance," or in some districts, under a provision of the federal Vocational Rehabilitation Act known as Section 504.

If one or more of these problems is showing up in your life and is getting in the way, you want to see what services your school district can offer. Birth disabilities like blindness, deafness, autism or Down syndrome are identified early on. But if a teenager has a slow loss of hearing or sight, no one may realize what is happening. Learning disabilities or emotional problems may not be apparent to others — or even to you.

Defining the Problem

To attack a problem successfully, you have to understand just what the need is. Sometimes all that is needed is a conference with teachers and counselor. Often, however, determining your needs will require diagnostic testing. I wish I could write that all schools understand this and are eager to help you discover and address your learning difficulties. Some schools work patiently with you to identify needed services, and if yours is one of them, you are lucky. In many districts, though, there are not enough qualified testers or enough resources to help students once a diagnostic test pinpoints a problem. You are going to need adults to help you if you are in this situation. One California expert who does private testing and evaluation observes bitterly that the shortage of resources is leading school administrators to be blatantly deceptive and to put economic interests before the good of the child.

Parents Must Be Involved

Here is some important advice you should share with your parents: they must be insistent and determined on your behalf. They must ask for a clear understanding of what is to happen and when and then insist that it happen. Each state interprets and implements federal guidelines differently, so parents must be familiar with the rules in their state as well as the provisions in the Individuals with Disabilities Education Act that protects students' rights. It is easy to lose your temper when you feel you are being driven crazy by bureaucracy, but it doesn't help. Knowing the district policy and holding people accountable does help.

Parents must also know when they are fighting a battle they are unlikely to win and when it is time to transfer energies to a more productive avenue. Some families decide to seek out a district that is known to provide especially appropriate education for students who have a specific need and figure out a way to move there.

Throughout the process of defining your problem and determining the solution, make copies of materials you provide, save copies of papers you are given, and ask for minutes from meetings in writing before you leave the meeting to make sure you have understood correctly. While parents are supposed to be given written summaries of meetings, you may want to write your own summary and send it to the special education counselor or school consultant to make sure everybody is reading from the same script. If it helps you, you may tape-record meetings.

A school district will do what it thinks right in terms of the greatest good for the greatest number. *A parent must advocate for what is right for one child.* Don't be embarrassed by a parent who disagrees with school officials. Your parents are supposed to stand up for your needs, and students who have parents who can do this are fortunate.

Testing

To decide if testing is necessary, there is generally a detailed process that students and parents go through, beginning with a committee reviewing your school record. You want to find out exactly what process — what rules and regulations — your school district follows. This should be written down with copies available for students and parents. It is likely the process involves several meetings. The law requires that parents be invited to all meetings in which decisions about you are being discussed. Parents must make it clear that they want to attend and expect to be notified in advance of all meetings. If they can't attend, they should insist the meeting be re-scheduled. The person who is most important in these meetings is your representative, and your parents may likely be your best representative. They may bring a friend or adviser if they wish. You should not assume that a person appointed by the school to represent you will be able to put your interests ahead of the school's, but neither should you dismiss the help such a person may be able to provide.

There is disagreement over whether or not students should attend all meetings. You have a legal right to be included in meetings and many schools want you to attend. Certainly, high school students are able to understand the issues and contribute insights to the discussion, but there is a danger in going to all meetings. The purpose of the initial evaluation meetings is to show why you are an unsuccessful student. This means that without any discussion of your positive qualities, negative statements may be made about you, not always with sensitivity or care, in order to establish that you deserve services. This kind of negative conversation can unfairly hurt your self-esteem and make you feel bad. Even high school students can be intimidated by the adults in the meeting and be unable to talk effectively. On the other hand, you are the one best positioned to give feedback on what works and doesn't work for you in the classroom. Be flexible about your role. Talk with your parents or your adviser and decide when your presence in these meetings will help you and when it may hurt you.

Often, your counselor or committee will first focus on ways to help you improve your performance that can be carried out by you and your teachers in the classes you currently attend. Having lectures taped, giving you more time to complete your work, providing written assignments each week, or other special services may be all that you need to find you are able to move forward successfully. Your school may recommend that you wait for testing until you find out if these new services are working for you. However, it is your right and your parents' right to request testing at any time.

Due to staff shortages, schools might subtly try to discourage parents from requesting diagnostic testing. "I know schools that are continually out of the form they require to order testing," one independent counselor explains. "Tell parents that the law gives them the right to initiate an assessment. If the school has a form, fill it out, but if they can't give you the form, take a piece of paper, date it, write down that you request the school do a complete assessment of your child to uncover his or her learning difficulties, and sign it. By law, the school is then held to a time line and must begin the process of evaluation." Remember to ask your parents to keep a copy of the school's form or their own written request.

Once a parent begins the process for assessment, the school must come up with an assessment plan that tells which tests it intends to administer to you. Your plan must be signed by the school and your parent. Before signing this plan, it is a very good idea to have a professional in the area review it to make sure that the school's plan will provide the kind of information that you need to figure out why you are having difficulties. If the school's testing is incomplete, you will not end up with the information you need to develop a corrective strategy.

Using Test Results to Develop an Educational Plan

Once you've completed the diagnostic tests, there must be a meeting in which the results of the tests and a written report about them are presented and reviewed by you and/or your representative(s) and the school's special education committee to determine whether you have a learning delay, a physical disability, or an emotional problem, and if so, what to do about it.

It may be difficult to determine the quality of the person who does the testing and evaluation. If the tester cannot explain the results so you or your parents understand them, keep asking questions and looking for additional explanations. Even though you may be unfamiliar with testing or teaching terms or special services, this does not make it all right for testers to explain things to other educators that are not clear to you. You and your parents are the people who most need to understand the results of the testing.

If you need special education services, you will be introduced to a world of alphabet soup in which diagnoses and treatments all seem to have abbreviations. What comes first is an IEP meeting to develop your Individual Education Plan. The first meeting to discuss this should occur no more than thirty days after you have been tested. The purpose of this meeting is to figure out what services you need to succeed academically, how to deliver these services to you and how to determine later on if you received the services recommended and if these services were helpful. Sometimes a draft plan is prepared before the meeting, but, in fact, the purpose of the meeting is to have a brainstorming session based on the information presented rather than to review the ideas of one person. Sometimes, in an effort to make sure all the right people are included in the discussion, the meeting room is crowded. If some attendees cannot contribute to your IEP and are weighing down the conversation, your representative may excuse them from the meeting. Also, you can request that certain persons attend the meeting — for example, the person who administered the tests.

At the end of an IEP meeting, you and your parents should have a clear description of baseline learning behavior, baseline scores, and educational goals. Your IEP plan will describe what should help you reach the improvements your representative(s) and the education committee are aiming for, ways to reach your goals, a timetable, and a schedule for putting the IEP into action.

The law says that an IEP meeting must occur at least once every year, but you or your representative can call a meeting as many times as you feel necessary, and the school should arrange it within thirty days of your request. Remember, according to law the student and/or his or her representative is in charge of this process, not the school. Don't let anyone convince you otherwise.

Parents or students may bring anyone they want to the meetings. (See the following section, Finding Expert Assistance.) If someone in the meeting needs an interpreter, ask the school to provide one. You must let the school know this ahead of time. Students under eighteen must have a parent or guardian present.

What the IEP outlines is what is supposed to happen for you. However, it may be necessary to be firm about insisting that the recommendations be carried out. Teachers are busy, schools are crowded, everyone is juggling lots of needs — and one child's problems can get overlooked.

Most students receive special education services in regular classes. Services can be provided in many different ways, for example, providing needed equipment, putting lectures on tape, and providing physical or speech therapy. But in order to get this support, you have to start the process.

Every student who receives special education services before high school will have, at age fourteen, an Individual Transition Plan (ITP) developed to plan for his or her transition from high school to college or work and life in the community. Parents and students participate in this planning as they do with the IEP.

Finding Expert Assistance

While some schools may resist testing or do a poor job, the alternative is too costly for most families. Private testing is expensive. A full battery of psychological and diagnostic tests can run well over $1,000. The most cost-efficient approach is to have the school district do an evaluation, as required by law. A good place to get expert help is in reviewing the proposed testing plan so you can be sure you will have enough information to diagnose the problem. In certain circumstances, when you or your parents disagree with the district's evaluation or recommendations, you may be entitled to district support in paying for an outside evaluation.

Once the tests are completed they must be interpreted, and again expert assistance may make the process more effective. If your family is able, it can be helpful to hire a private consultant who specializes in learning disabilities to be an advocate along with your parents. You can ask this consultant to review the proposed assessment plan and then to attend the IEP meetings and participate in developing recommendations for special services and for later evaluation of the plan. Or you can go further and have this person observe you in classes, review your records, and examine your schoolwork to help you decide what is getting in your way of learning. This is an excellent beginning for an IEP process. You can find qualified people who will visit your school and observe and attend meetings on an hourly basis. This process will cost several hundred dollars.

It will be a great benefit to you to find someone who knows the law, knows your district, and knows the testing instruments. If your family cannot afford outside help, your parents may want to connect with another parent who has been through the process and is willing to help you learn the ropes. Each state has a federally funded Parent Information and Training Center which offers training on student rights and on the best strategies for obtaining special services.

One of the many good places to look for help is the Learning Disability Association of America. Founded in 1963, it now has six hundred chapters around the country and is the largest support group for disabilities in this country. It is devoted to defining and finding solutions for the broad spectrum of learning problems. The association can put you in touch with a chapter in your city. If there isn't one, they will put you in touch with the state chapter. This is a way to plug into a network of parents, teens, and experts who can help you figure out what is going on with you. If no one in your area has experience with your problem, they will help you research additional information and expertise. To contact the Learning Disability Association of America, write to 4156 Library Rd., Pittsburgh, PA 15234, or call (412) 341-1515. Fax: (412) 344-0224.

When parents or you yourself discover that you have a learning delay or physical disability in high school, it's a good idea to find out if there is a family support group where you and your parents can learn from the experiences of others. Usually, these groups are free. If you can't find a group, ask around in your circle for other families that have a similar situation or contact the Learning Disability Association of America (see above). Another good resource is the Orton Society in Baltimore, which addresses all types of learning disabilities. Their number is (410) 296-0232.

Remember, there are bound to be others who have the same concerns as you do, and talking with people who have been there before you can help enormously. There is no reason to feel embarrassed by any kind of physical or emotional problem that trips you up. Much better to shine a bright light on it, look at it carefully, and figure out how to shrink its impact.

When Testing Is Not Required

There is another good reason that schools may be reluctant to provide testing. Sometimes it seems very clear to everyone outside your family circle that the problem getting in the way of school performance has to do with your family dynamics instead of a learning delay, but adults in your family may not want to hear this.

A clinical psychologist in California told me an interesting story. One day she received a rather frantic call from concerned parents. It seems their son had been failing a class each year since freshman year and now, as a senior, he was in danger of not graduating. Could she see them immediately for a consultation? She made an appointment and asked the parents to bring their son's transcript. After meeting the family briefly and looking at the transcript, she asked to chat with the boy alone.

"Well," she said, "this is a really interesting transcript, and I am eager to hear your story."

"What story?" he asked.

"Each year you have failed a different class in a completely different subject area — and all your other grades are quite good. Seems to me it has taken some effort to make this happen. It's no accident. So I'm curious about the message you are trying to send."

In one minute it was out on the table: "My parents insist that only good grades are acceptable, and they want to dictate to me how I am going to perform in high school."

Control, not academics, was the issue on this table.

Personal problems can get in the way — big time — of your school performance. If you have a learning delay or physical disability that results from the way your body is wired, odds are that it will have shown up before high school. Dyslexia (trouble reading), dyscalculia (trouble with math), dysgraphia (trouble with writing), attention deficit syndrome, and auditory processing problems — the most common learning disabilities — usually appear long before high school. It is possible that you are so successful or adept interpersonally that you have managed to hang on in elementary school and middle school but can no longer ignore learning problems in high school. If this is the case, however, you usually will see, in looking back, some evidence of a learning problem.

If there is nothing in your past to suggest a learning disability and if a careful physical exam shows no physical basis for a pronounced change in your school performance, it makes sense to think about an emotional upset. However, before you conclude your problem is emotional, make sure that it is not physical.

You may be reluctant to talk about emotional problems for all sorts of reasons. Sometimes teens feel ashamed, they don't want to burden their parents, they don't think their parents will be able to help, they think their parents will be disappointed in them, they think they should be able to work it out themselves, they don't want to implicate friends, or they have been told they or their families will be hurt if they report something. These are all important issues, but they are not reasons to keep your troubles all locked up inside of you. It is very difficult to deal with problems that we can't discuss and look at from many different angles.

It may be that as you understand more about yourself, you and your family can find ways to talk more intimately and comfortably. This comes slowly sometimes, but with patience and persistence, many teens have discovered solutions to problems they previously thought unsolveable. Maybe a relative or family friend can be a listening post or your school can provide counseling support to help you with this work. Sometimes, it is a good idea to spend money on an experienced outsider — a therapist who can create a safe, danger-free zone in which you are able to speak freely. Visiting a therapist does not mean there is anything wrong with you or your family. We see doctors to make sure we are not seriously sick and we see lawyers to make sure we don't do anything that will get us in trouble. And we can go to see a therapist to keep from getting into an emotional box. A little bit of help from someone with a fresh perspective can sometimes put you back on track before one problem creates another.

Special Schools

If you have a disability that cannot be served in regular high schools, your district may have a special school for you or may pay tuition for a private school or public school in a neighboring district. Current legislation requires schools to "include" students (formerly called mainstreaming) whenever possible — that is, to keep them in a regular school classroom. While this policy works for the majority of students, it sometimes causes problems for others. Some schools simply cannot provide the kind of support you require. A once-a-week session with a special teacher may be all the school can offer for you, though you would benefit from more intensive services. Your district may place you in a regular school though you'd prefer a specialized program. Many districts believe that mainstreaming provides better life skills than a special school. Sometimes, a district may want to keep a special education student in regular classes but in a school that is not where everyone else in the neighborhood goes. If it's hard to get to know other kids in your neighborhood, ask for services at your local school.

It helps to have a chance to leave the school environment in which problems are occurring and to spend time in a school that is organized entirely to provide special education services for students with a particular delay or disability. Your school district may offer such schools, or you may consider a private school for a time. Many years ago, I worked in education in St. Louis. I remember talking with parents and students who had left their schools for a year or two to attend the Churchill School, a private school designed to help children with dyslexia and related learning disabilities, to develop coping strategies that they could take back to their regular schools. Both students and parents spoke with great relief and appreciation for what Churchill was accomplishing in teaching them. One young man explained that he had always felt dumb before coming to Churchill. I remember his saying something like this:

> My parents told me I was smart, but I knew they were just telling me that to make me feel better. I knew I was stupid because I couldn't do what my friends could do in school. For the first time in my life, I believe I am smart. I know I am going to have to work harder than my friends because schoolwork takes me longer, but I am learning how to do it here in ways that work for me. I hate this school sometimes because they demand so much, but really, I love this school.

It is difficult to figure out the best educational strategy for students with special needs. Parents who are equally devoted to and involved with their children can make very different choices. For example, some parents of deaf children concentrate on helping the child to speak and lip-read and discourage sign language, while others want their child to become adept at sign language and therefore look for opportunities for the child to interact with other deaf teens. Parents and teens together must gather all the information they can and make the decisions that seem right for their specific situation.

16. Extracurricular Activities

Do you remember how Chapter 10, What Does It Mean to Be "Smart" and How Do You Get Smarter?, talked about the different kinds of intelligences? Your extracurricular activities develop different parts of you, different aspects of your intelligence, than your school classes. Wise teens hunt out activities that let them use their favorite kinds of intelligence or help develop sides of themselves they want to be stronger.

Whether you decide to build your strengths or your less-developed skills, find activities that sound like fun. In classes, you get graded on how well you do. In after-school activities, interest counts as well as ability, and there are no grades. While some schools require passing grades to play on school teams and participate in school activities, there are many community activities in which grades don't matter.

What to Do?

There are clubs, teams, groups, or organizations for every kind of interest. For example, if you love sports and aren't good enough for a varsity team, find a club team, a church team, or a community league and play for the fun of it. If you aren't big enough for football, try lacrosse, which is just as competitive but has room for smaller players. If you aren't tall enough for varsity basketball, start a game for short shooters. Sing in a chorus, play in a band, or learn an instrument. Act in plays, help paint the backdrop, collect the props, or make the costumes. Dance, exercise, practice yoga, learn to be a clown, help in a community garden, or lift weights. Bike, hike, or learn to high dive. Make jewelry, throw pots, paint pictures, carve wood, or turn junk into sculpture. Repair cars, race cars, make models or be a model. Yodel, hurdle, clog, or collect something. Join a language club, a computer club, a chess club, or a writing group. Pick a sport — any sport, an art form — any form.

Local religious groups, community centers, and recreation facilities all have activities to offer you. Boy Scouts, coed Explorer Scouts, and Girl Scouts offer great opportunities. It is not too late to get involved in scouting as a teen. Community groups focused on special interests — for example, model railroading, chess, theater, or square dancing — are always looking for new people. There are hundreds of volunteer jobs that really need you. Talk with lonely seniors, play with little kids, help out in an animal shelter or work on a political campaign, to name just a few choices. Read the bulletin boards at school and your local weekly newspapers for other ideas.

Many cities have *volunteer centers* that match volunteers with the right activity. Many serve the surrounding region as well. If your city is not listed in the box provided here, look under the heading Volunteer Center in the phone book or call your local United Way. The United Way information desk will be able to tell you if there is an independent volunteer center in your community or if the United Way runs a volunteer matching service. If neither of these are in place, your local United Way should be able to direct you to community groups in your area that use volunteers. Volunteer centers will work with you to find the right volunteer position for you. They will ask you what interests you, what area of the city is convenient for you, and what times you want to volunteer. Then they will search their database and give you, when possible, several volunteer opportunity suggestions.

Are You Shy or Reluctant?

Don't worry about whether you are "good enough" to get involved. Everyone is good enough. Get up the gumption to make the first move, which is simply to call the right person, and say, "Hi. I think I would like to do this." When you join a group that has been together for a

Volunteer Centers

Albuquerque, NM	(505) 247-3671	Louisville, KY*	(502) 583-2822
Atlanta, GA*	(404) 527-3591	Memphis, TN	(901) 579-2261
Austin, TX	(512) 472-3848	Miami, FL*	(305) 579-2261
Baltimore, MD*	(410) 547-8000 x513	Minneapolis, MN*	(612) 340-7449
Birmingham, AL*	(205) 251-5131	New Orleans,	(504) 488-4636
Boise, ID*	(208) 354-4357	LA	
Boston, MA*	(617) 422-6765	Oklahoma City,	(405) 232-3711
Charlotte, NC*	(704) 371-7170	OK	
Chicago, IL*	(312) 906-2424	Omaha, NE*	(402) 342-8232 x531
Dallas, TX	(214) 826-6767		
Denver, CO*	(303) 894-0103	Philadelphia,	(215) 665-2474
Des Moines, IA*	(515) 246-6540	PA*	
Fairbanks, AK	(907) 452-7000	Phoenix, AZ	(602) 263-9736 x877
Houston, TX	(281) 461-9152		
Honolulu, HI*	(808) 536-7234	Portland, ME	(207) 874-1000
Indianapolis, IN*	(317) 921-1275	St. Louis, MO*	(314) 539-4063
Kansas City, KS*	(913) 371-3674	Salt Lake City,	(801) 978-2452
Las Vegas, NV*	(702) 892-2320	UT	
Little Rock, AR*	(501) 376-4567	San Jose, CA	(408) 247-1126
Pittsburgh, PA*	(412) 450-6841	Seattle, WA*	(206) 461-3706
Los Angeles, CA	(213) 484-2849		

*Volunteer center is under the auspices of the United Way.

while, it's natural to feel like an outsider at first. Give it time. Be persistent, don't give up, tolerate a little normal discomfort, and soon it will start to feel familiar. Don't rule activities out because you are shy. Extracurricular activities are an ideal way for shy people to meet others and develop better social skills. Working together on projects or activities often leads to friendships.

If you are hesitant about becoming involved in extracurricular activities, think about some of the good reasons to do this:

1. It's fun.
2. You become a more interesting person.
3. You make new friends.
4. You learn new skills.
5. Serious participation in activities appeals to employers, scholarship committees, and college admissions committees.
6. Skills you develop in extracurricular activities can help in the job world and even lead you to a career.

College Benefits

Highly competitive colleges look at students' extracurricular activities as well as their academics. If you apply to one of these colleges, you will be competing with students who offer more than good grades. It's better to have a few activities that you've been involved in consistently and to which you've made real contributions than to have a long list of clubs you joined but haven't really participated in. It is impressive — and satisfying — to have created something new, improved something old or organized a project that has a positive effect on the community. Admissions officers are interested in students who solo in the choir and teach gymnastics or who volunteer with senior citizens and also campaign for environmental controls and play soccer. But you don't have to be a jack-of-all-trades. If you have one strong interest, follow it and become an important contributor in that area.

Reasons Students Don't Get Involved

Many schools have late buses for students who are involved in after-school activities or student-organized car pools, so don't let transportation keep you from being active. And don't be afraid to join a club or group because you don't know anyone who is already involved. All those

If It's Worth Doing, Is It Always Worth Doing Well?

It feels odd to be warning against excellence when I usually support it — but many teens find themselves in situations where a caution is needed. There is a growing and disquieting trend toward competitive superiority in extracurricular activities. The sports coaches tell students, "We expect your all." Choirmasters and orchestra directors explain that members must be prepared to give their full commitment to all practices and performances, or otherwise shouldn't be involved. The yearbook is out to win awards, and so is the newspaper, the debate team, and the drama club. There is nothing wrong with this. It's fun to compete and achieve, and there are wonderful lessons to be learned by aiming for the top and working relentlessly to get there.

However, you cannot give your all to every activity; sometimes, "just enough" is the right amount. It is better, for example, to have the fun of singing with a group that simply enjoys making music than to give up singing entirely because you can't attend every rehearsal of the choir that aims to win awards. In choosing extracurricular activities, strike a balance. Pick what is most important for your best efforts, and then look for outlets to express other parts of yourself that put enjoyment over excellence. If your parents are urging you to put a little more balance or a little less pressure in your life, they may have a point. On the other hand, if "just enough" is your measure for all activities and you avoid reaching for excellence in any arena, then you need to adjust in the other direction.

people who are now participating were new themselves once. If you are hesitant to go alone, try to talk a friend into joining you, or approach a student who is already active and ask if he or she might help you. Another strategy is to talk with the adult adviser about introducing you to the group. If you have trouble scheduling an appointment with the adviser, send a note explaining that you're interested in figuring out a way to get involved.

Parents should not be deciding your extracurricular activities, but a parental nudge here and there is often helpful. Your parents know you well, and it's worth considering their ideas and even following their lead on occasion. My older son teased me about doing much more than nudging him to join the stage crew at his school. He eventually gave the idea a chance, and he found something he enjoyed a great deal that led to opportunities neither of us imagined at the time.

Sometimes, after-school jobs keep you from extracurricular activities. That's one good reason to get involved in the ninth grade, when you're less likely to have paid employment. Later, you can decide which will be more satisfying for you — working at a paying job or participating fully in extracurricular activities. Maybe you can manage your schedule to include both.

Pick something. Jump in. Make it work for you. Enjoy it!

17. Why College?

If you have known since grade school that you were college-bound and you have been doing everything you need to do to get there, skip this chapter and start reading Chapter 19, Which College? But if you're not sure about college, read this chapter carefully!

College isn't for everyone; less than 25 percent of Americans have a four-year college degree. But it *is* for some teens who don't go, and it isn't for some who do.

About 60 percent of high school graduates go directly into a college program. About half of those, 30 percent, come out the other end with a four-year degree. That means that seven out of every ten high school graduates need an alternative plan for what to do after high school. There are a variety of ways to move from school to work, and college is not the best solution for all students.

The decision is not as simple as saying "Yes, I want to go to college" or "No, I don't want to go to college." There are about 1,700 four-year colleges and 1,660 two-year colleges in the U.S.; they offer all kinds of choices. Some college programs avoid specific career preparation; others are emphatically focused on preparing students for a particular field. These are *very* different choices. You can be miserable in one place and wonderfully happy in another. You can find yourself motivated and eager to study in a school that is right for you and depressed and disorganized in a school that doesn't suit you. Rather than beginning with the question, "Do I want to go to college?," you and your parents should be asking, "How do I learn best and what do I want to learn?"

It is never too late to decide to attend college. There is no age limit. You can start college at any time. Some people need to get out in the work world in order to appreciate the benefits of a college education. Your parents may worry that once you get out of the habit of school, you won't go back. It can be hard to get back into the school groove once you have left it — but if you have no idea why you are in college or what you want from it, it will be difficult to study no matter when you go.

If you're not planning to go to college right after high school, ask yourself every year "Am I ready to go back to school?" Remember that going to college doesn't have to mean going for a degree. We can all take college courses or noncredit continuing education classes just because they teach something we want to learn. And "going back" doesn't have to mean going to college. There are many ways to keep learning and to prepare for work besides the traditional college route. See the next chapter, Where to Go for Job Training.

Why Some Choose Not to Go to College

College may or may not be the right choice for you. What is important is that you reject or select it using *good sense* and *fact*, not wishful thinking or hearsay. Half the students who enroll in college expecting to earn a bachelor's degree drop out. Students who drop out and have no work skills may find themselves less well positioned than students who went directly into a career-oriented training program.

Five-year-olds running in the playground cannot imagine how they will feel at fifteen. Ninth graders are wiser than five-year-olds. High school seniors are wiser yet, but still can't imagine how they will feel at thirty or fifty. The way you see the world now is not the way you will see it later. If you think this is inaccurate advice, ask twenty people over the age of thirty if they think their judgment at eighteen was as good as it is now.

When Do You Decide About College? One reason students don't continue on to college is that they don't think about it until graduation is staring them in the face. Suddenly you're a senior, and college seems a lot more interesting to you than it did in ninth grade.

Eight *Good* Reasons Not to Go to College

1. I have always been a poor student. I don't believe I will be able to do well in college. Instead I have a plan to develop a career for myself.
2. I need more education but I want time to develop a better attitude as a student and get some real-world experience before continuing on with my formal education.
3. I have lined up an apprenticeship program that suits my needs.
4. I am going into the military and I have a clear plan for how it will further my education.
5. I am going to a technical or trade school or certificate program instead of a program aimed at a college degree.
6. I have a good job that will provide me with ongoing training.
7. I have been accepted to college but am deferring my admission for a year to travel.
8. I have been accepted to college but am deferring to work for one year to save money.

If you messed up in high school, you haven't cut yourself off from a college education. Many colleges have an open-door policy. This means that anyone with a high school diploma or GED can apply at any time. The college will give you the opportunity to take special noncredit classes to make up any math, reading or writing skills you missed in high school. It's hard to go back and fill in the academic holes, but the community colleges will help you if you want it badly enough.

You don't have to choose between career training and college courses in ninth or tenth grade. It is possible to do both and end up with good work skills *and* the grades and courses to do college work. The new Tech Prep programs are designed specifically to combine these goals. On the other hand, if your school record indicates that school doesn't bring out your best, don't fool yourself into thinking that college will

Nine Bad Reasons for Rejecting a College Education

1. My parents didn't go to college and they did O.K.
   Times are changing. Want to give up your VCR because your parents didn't have one?
2. I am smart enough that I don't need school.
   You may be right about being smart, but this statement does not sound smart.
3. I can't wait any longer to have money in my pocket.
   If you can put off having money now, odds are that, in the long run, you will end up with more money because you got a college education. This is called delayed gratification, and it is a characteristic of very successful people.
4. People like me don't belong in college.
   Every kind of person shows up in college. There is no racial, religious, financial, or ethnic reason not to go to college.
5. I can't afford college.
   Maybe you can! In many cities, it's possible to attend the com-

continued on next page

cure you of the academic blues. Go back and look at Chapter 12, Using School to Start Your Career.

You Have to Dream Imagine yourself five or ten years from now. Imagine the work you want to be doing, the setting in which you want to be working, the skills you want to possess. Imagine college as one way to get to there. If this picture seems bleak, look around for other possibilities to imagine. There are lots of exciting and mind-stretching alternatives to four years of college. Mr. Lindsey, who teaches pipe fitting and plumbing at Milby High School in Houston, notes sadly, "Our kids are lacking dreams." Dreaming is an equal opportunity activity. Every-

munity college as a full-time student for between $1,000 and $2,000 a year. With work, savings, Pell grants for low-income students, and loans, this is a choice open to most citizens. Ask for waiver of the fee for all college tests and for the application fee to colleges if you can't afford these. See the financial aid section in the next chapter.

6. I am too lazy to bother with all that.

   If this is the case, the odds are that you'll be too lazy to be successful. Usually, when people decide something is good for them, they can overcome laziness.

7. I am getting married so I don't need school.

   "Married" is about whom you live with. "School" is about training your brain. One has nothing to do with the other. If you think getting married means you can count on someone else's money, you may find you've been badly misinformed.

8. I am married or a parent and need to work to provide for our needs.

   With an education, it will be easier to fulfill your financial responsibilities in the years ahead. You may have to juggle to make college work for you, but perhaps you can do it. Some colleges have special dorms for single parents.

9. I don't like to plan. Things will work out.

   Don't count on it.

one can do it. It's free and easy and can be done any time. Once you have a dream, you can begin to use parts of your dream to develop a plan for yourself.

Sometimes teens have bold dreams, but they are dreams about romance, not education. Maybe you want to remain at home or go to only one place because that's where the love of your life is going. It is generally unwise to limit your dreams at eighteen in order to fit into someone else's dreams. Love is wonderful; love is delicious — but it lasts longer and more easily grows stronger when each of the people in love is happy in life. The best way to prepare for a good life with a mate is to take time to mature in your emotions and your career. Don't put aside good educational opportunities at eighteen only to stay close to a boyfriend or girlfriend. If that person is mature and truly cares for you and your future together, he or she will want you to take advantage of the best training opportunities you have. If each of you invests in yourselves, when you do come together you'll be bringing so much more to the relationship and increasing its chances for success.

You Must Implement the Dream You can't wish yourself into college — or into a job, a technical school, an apprenticeship, or the military. You must actually fill out the applications. You should be doing this during the first semester of your senior year. For students who decide against college, read the next chapter, Where to Go for Job Training. If college seems like a good choice, you will want to read Chapter 19, Which College?

Talking with Parents

How to Get the Discussion Going Here are nine true or false questions that you might find helpful in beginning a discussion with your parents about college. These questions are meant to help bring your feelings and concerns out on the table. This works best if you and your parents answer the questions separately and then compare your answers.

1. Pleasing parents is a good reason for going to college.
2. There are other equally good ways besides college to continue an education and shape a work life.
3. We will be able to figure out how to afford college.
4. It is important to know what you want from college before you begin.
5. The direction my life is going to take in terms of career is fairly clear.
6. People who don't go to college are never going to command respect in the working world.

7. It is better to start college and drop out than to choose another alternative first.
8. Traditional academic settings work well for me.
9. College is important, but in my case might best be postponed.

If you are undecided about what to do, it may be reasonable to try college because your parents urge you to do so. If you have no desire to spend another year in a traditional classroom, however, it may be far wiser to explore other alternatives with your parents. A good solution for some teens is to arrange for college attendance but to take a year off before beginning college. A book that may help you with this decision is called *Taking Time Off* by Colin Hall and Ron Lieber.

I know that in advising my sons, I always wanted good things for them. In deciding what was "good," however, I had mostly my own experiences to guide me. Things that were good for me or that I had always thought would be good for me but never had the chance to do, I tended to think might be good for them. Experiences that were not good for me I recommended against. I did not encourage those things I knew nothing about or that scared me. That's not a bad strategy — except that my sons are not me. And, as you can imagine, they had their own ideas about what would be good for them. Fortunately, we were able to sit at the table, put everybody's ideas out for examination and talk and research our way through to good decisions. My sons were able to help me in this because, when they disagreed with something I or their father proposed, they were usually willing to talk about why they didn't think it was a good idea. Sometimes they changed their minds; just as often we changed ours.

If you and your parents can develop comfortable ways of communicating, you will reach better decisions and enjoy family life more. You have to help with this process. Some teens do have parents who have trouble listening or understanding. More often, however, they have parents who love them fiercely, know them well, and are trying hard to give good direction and support. Maybe you have to help educate your parents in certain areas as they have helped to educate you. Maybe you have to bring new information to them to help them understand your point of view. Maybe they have ideas that are worth considering. Don't make your parents your adversaries. There are most likely few other people who care about you as much as they do. Make them your allies.

18. Where to Go for Job Training

High school graduation is cause for celebration. When you walk down the aisle and pick up that diploma, you are finished with high school. And if you are wise, you won't be finished with your formal training. All the information on labor market projections for the years in which you will be working suggest that the smart next move for you, if you are not continuing on to college, is job training.

Many different ideas may be rushing through your mind. Maybe you're eager to put studying behind you. Perhaps you are focused on earning a steady paycheck so you can afford an apartment of your own. Maybe you have a job but aren't sure whether it's the best job for you. I hope that as you approach graduation you worry less about making good money now and more about gaining additional job skills that can help you build a successful career over time.

I recommend this because in the twenty-first century, the demand for employees with little or no job training after high school will decline. The greatest growth area will be in work that requires two or more years of formal education after high school but not necessarily a four-year college degree. Dr. Kenneth B. Hoyt, who is developing a program (Counseling for High Skills) at Kansas State University that's designed to help teens and young adults make intelligent career and training choices, warns, "This society calls for almost all high school leavers to secure some form of postsecondary education if they hope to gain access to and participate in the primary labor market." When Dr. Hoyt and others who study the labor market look at the statistics, they report that the greatest job growth is going to be with jobs requiring two or more years of post–high school training, but not necessarily a four-year degree.

As you approach your high school graduation, you want to be thinking about where you might go to get the kinds of training that will prepare you for good jobs with good wages in the years ahead. Take some time to go on a fact-finding mission. Look for careers that take advantage of your strengths and capture your interest and find out what kind of training they require. Just as seniors looking for colleges are advised to be open-minded, talk with many people, ask questions and gather lots of information, so also must students who are going to prepare for work without getting a four-year degree.

There are six kinds of places that can help you get job training:

Community College Programs Community colleges offer two kinds of programs: a two-year associate degree program and a certificate program. A two-year associate degree program gives you a community college degree and prepares you either to continue on to a four-year college or enter the job market. While associate degrees require core academic credits, including English and math, most are specifically career-oriented. For example, the community college catalog on my desk describes programs in audio and recording technology, nursing, building science, insurance and risk management, material management, child development, commercial art, court reporting, dietetic technology, fire protection technology, and fashion design — to name some of the possibilities. Once you complete your core requirements, you can focus on classes designed to prepare you for work.

Certificate (or diploma) programs usually last less than two years and are more job-oriented. They are intended to prepare you for entry-level jobs in specific career areas. A look in the same catalog shows, for example, that you can become certified in emergency medical technology by taking ten classes offered over three semesters. (Semester hours are based on how many hours per week a class meets each semester. A two-semester-hour class will meet two hours per week for one semester. Tuition is often calculated on a semester-hour basis.)

Your community college may also offer clock-hour certificates. Traditionally, these have been recognized in a specific industry or trade as the credential you need to get an advanced position. For example, a person interested in auto-body work could be awarded an auto-body repair certificate by spending 1,440 hours in a combination of theory and hands-on classes. Many people enroll in certificate programs on a part-time basis while working in a related job.

You can complete most certificate programs in one year of study or less; some are only a few weeks long. Many certificate programs do not require any of the academic courses that are required for an associate degree, but if you need or want to take these courses, community colleges usually offer their students a variety of study supports to help them master difficult classes.

Get a catalog from your community college. Make sure you have a catalog that lists courses for *all* campuses. Look through it, considering both associate degree and certificate classes. You might want to start with the index at the back of the book to get a quick overview. Decide what interests you and set up an appointment with the person in charge of each program for which you would like more information or with a community college counselor.

For more comprehensive information, check out *Peterson's Guide to Vocational and Technical Schools*, *Peterson's Guide to Two-Year Colleges*, or *Peterson's Guide to Certificate Programs at American Colleges and Universities*. These books are available in the library or your local bookstore. You can order directly by calling 1-800-338-3282.

Community colleges usually serve specified geographic districts within your state. If you live in that district, you pay the in-district cost for each college credit or semester hour. If you live out of the district you can still attend that college, but you will pay the out-of-district tuition. Costs vary around the country. In 1996, for example, at Philadelphia Community College, Philadelphia in-district students paid $228 for three credits and $899 for twelve or more credits. In-state students who lived outside the district paid double, and out-of-state students paid triple. Students at the Community College of Southern Nevada, which is open to all Nevada residents, paid $109.50 for three credits or $458 for a full load. Out-of-state students paid $51.50 per credit for the first six credits or $1,650 plus the in-state rate of $36.50 per credit if taking more than six credits. At all colleges, you will also have to pay fees and buy books.

Your community college may have several campuses, and all courses may not be offered on every campus. In some circumstances, it may be a good idea for you to pay the out-of-district cost at a community college in a neighboring district or go to a campus that is less conveniently located because it offers the best program for you. It makes sense to pay a little more money to get what you need than to save money taking classes that are not geared to your interests. Ask people who are successful in the field in which you plan to study where to find the best programs. Go to your high school counselor's office or the downtown library and look at the catalogs from all the schools in your area or pick up copies for yourself.

Financial aid, in the form of grants or loans, is available for students who want certificates and associate degrees. Every community college has a financial aid counselor who can help you determine if you qualify.

Apprentice Programs Registered apprenticeship programs combine job experience with training. They offer high-level skills training, rotation through all aspects of a trade or industry, a good understanding of safety and accident prevention on the job, and the probability of higher earnings. Apprenticeship programs are run jointly by employers and their employer associations or unions or by employers alone.

If you choose this training route after high school, you will be working hard because you will have to attend classes outside of working hours that complement the work you are doing. Most registered apprenticeships require about three thousand to six thousand hours of supervised on-the-job training plus 144 hours of classroom instruction. When you complete a registered apprenticeship program, you receive a certificate from the Department of Labor that is recognized and respected nationally. Some jobs are open only to people with these certificates, and some offer higher pay to employees who are certified.

The largest concentration of apprenticeships are in the building and construction trades followed by manufacturing, but more than eight hundred types of programs around the country have been recognized by the Department of Labor or a state apprenticeship agency. Approximately four hundred currently take apprentices. Many of the programs are small, but there *are* spaces available if you go looking. You must be determined in tracking down information about programs in areas that interest you. Ask lots of people for information, especially people who have already completed programs.

Some programs are only open in-house to employees already working for a company. Others are advertised in the newspaper, and you just have to be on the look out for these ads. The largest number of apprentice slots will be found in union-sponsored programs. If you decide there is a union program that is right for you, put your name on that union's apprenticeship mailing list so you receive the latest information about openings.

It is an asset to know people established in an area, but you do not have to be "connected" to get an apprenticeship slot. There are between 250,000 and 300,000 slots available in the U.S., and all of those who fill them don't have family connections. While discrimination issues linger in dark corners of the country, race, gender, and religion are less important than ability, interest, and commitment. Timing is important, too. Some programs accept applicants only once a year for a few weeks, so find out in advance the who/what/when/how details for occupations on your list.

Most apprentice programs require that you take and pass an eligibility

Bureau of Apprenticeship and Training Regional Offices

Location

Region I
JFK Federal Building
Boston, MA 02203
(617) 565-2288

States Served
CT, NH, ME, MA, RI, VT

Region II
Room 602—Federal Building
201 Varick Street
New York, NY 10014
(212) 337-2313

NJ, NY, PR, U.S. Virgin Islands

Region III
Room 13240—Gateway Building
3535 Market Street
Philadelphia, PA 19104
(215) 596-6417

DE, MD, PA, VA, WV

Region IV
Room 200
1371 Peachtree St. NE
Atlanta, GA 30367
(404) 347-4405

AL, FL, GA, KY, MS, NC, SC, TN

Region V
Room 708
230 South Dearborn St.
Chicago, IL 60604
(312) 353-7205

IL, IN, MI, MN, OH, WI

continued on next page

Location	States Served
Region VI Room 628 — Federal Building Dallas, TX 75202 (214) 767-4993	AL, LA, NM, OK, TX
Region VII Suite 1040 Main St. Kansas City, MO 64105 (816) 426-3856	IA, KS, MO, NE
Region VIII Room 465 — U.S. Customs House 721 19th St. Denver, CO 80202 (303) 844-4791	CO, MT, ND, SD, UT, WY
Region IX Federal Building, Room 715 71 Stevenson St. San Francisco, CA 94105 (415) 744-6580	AZ, CA, HI, NV
Region X Room 925 1111 Third Ave. Seattle, WA 98101 (201) 553-5286	AK, ID, OR, WA

test to be considered for entry to the program. If you pass the test you will probably be interviewed, and your high school transcript will be reviewed. In many trades, you will need a decent grasp of math to pass the eligibility test, so you may want to buy a review book and brush up beforehand.

Many apprenticeship programs are affiliated with local community colleges, and you can talk with people there in the program area that interests you. Some employers with apprentice slots recruit through community colleges because they can reach potential apprentices who have shown an interest in the field by signing up for related classes. Also, call the local union or independent trade association for the kind of work that interests you and ask if there is an apprentice program. Or find someone working in that trade — a career or technology education teacher at school may be able to help you — and go to them for advice.

To find the nearest Department of Labor apprenticeship counselor, you can check with your regional office for the Bureau of Apprenticeship and Training. Or try the national School-to-Work Learning and Information Center at 1-800-251-7236. If you can't make a local contact with a union, call the international headquarters or the AFL/CIO in Washington, D.C., at (202) 637-5000.

Don't get discouraged if you have difficulty reaching the right person. Keep calling until you connect with the person who can help you. It wasn't easy for me to track down the people whom I needed to speak to when I was researching this book, so if you have difficulty, don't assume it is a personal rejection. If you leave a message and don't get a call back, just keep calling. If you finally contact the right person and they seem to put you off, don't give up. Ask these questions:

- When are you taking applications for apprenticeships?
- What is the selection procedure?
- Is there anything I can do to prepare myself to do well in the selection process?
- How many people will you accept in your program?
- Do you know about other apprentice programs in this industry that might be taking in people now?

Dale Shoemaker, technical coordinator for the International Carpenters' Union apprenticeship programs, recalls that when he was a young man with a year of college engineering and lots of millwright experience in the military, he tried to get an apprenticeship slot with the mill workers. "I'd call and they'd say to call back in a few months. I called every two weeks for two years until I got the job. Tell young people that persistence is a key in getting what you want."

The International Carpenters' Union, for example, currently has 35,000 people in apprenticeship programs nationally. About 10,000 new apprentices will join their programs in the coming year. Shoemaker says his union is eager to take in young workers recently graduated from high school who can be trained with the most advanced technologies. "Tell them not to pass up an apprenticeship program in order to start out making a few bucks an hour more with some contractor who is going to keep them doing the same job over and over."

Dr. Robert Glover, who works at the Center for the Study of Human Resources at the University of Texas at Austin, has studied apprenticeship programs here and in other countries. He states, "Apprenticeships offer learners an ideal training system providing earning while learning, practical training on the job combined with theoretical studies, and a natural environment for mentoring." Research on the construction industry shows, he says, "that craft workers who complete apprenticeships tend to work more steadily, earn more, and advance to supervisory positions faster than individuals trained in other ways."

Private Technical, Trade, and Business Schools There are, all over the country, private technical, trade, and business schools that can be excellent places to acquire skills that are in demand in the job market. The mission of these schools is to put you to work, not to prepare you for a college degree. If you are thinking about continuing on with a four-year college degree, you may want to focus on community college classes that will transfer for credit, but if you're looking for the fastest route to a good job, consider the private technical, trade, or business schools. Private schools may be able to train you faster than community colleges and provide more help with job placement.

Steve Greg, a director with the Art Institutes, International, which has professional schools throughout the country, says, "If you enroll, I am required by law to offer you a series of courses that will get you out in the shortest time possible." In community colleges, you may find that the classes you need to take are full or are not being offered the semester you want them. Greg says that technical schools must provide the classes you need when you need them. The only way private schools can compete in the marketplace, he explains, is to ensure that students do well in the program, graduate on schedule, find jobs, and tell others how satisfied they were.

> We are a business, so why would I enroll a student who is going to be a failure and then go out and represent us in the community? My graduates are my products, the proof of what we do here. I don't want students to just enroll and stay a quarter or two. I want them to stay and graduate. I am monitored by every kind of agency, and they evaluate me based on my graduation rates.

To find a school that is right for you, do your homework and investigate carefully. To learn about local options, look in the yellow pages under Schools for the subsections titled Schools — Business and Secretarial and Schools — Industrial and Technical and Trade. For a look at your choices nationally, check out *Peterson's Guide to Vocational and Technical Schools* (in two volumes — schools in the East and schools in the West). Remember that requesting information, visiting, and asking questions cost next to nothing.

Visit any program you are considering. Spend several hours or even the whole day observing classes, evaluating teachers, and talking with students. Ask for the names of graduates. Find out from former students how much job-placement assistance the school provides. You can certainly visit more than once. Find out if this is a school that does what it promises by speaking to students who have gone through the program.

You will also want to learn how many students who begin the program graduate from it and how many graduates are in jobs related to their training within three months after they graduate. The schools are required to keep statistics on program completion and job placement rates, so don't feel shy about asking. Ask how large your classes will be and the maximum number of students in a class. Smaller classes are usually better for students. There is some evidence to suggest, in fact, that students who go to smaller schools (less than three hundred students) have a higher rate of graduation. Find out the median starting salary of the school's graduates and the five-year income average of those still in the industry.

Ask what the policy is if you decide to drop out of the program. Typically you lose a semester of tuition but you do not lose the entire cost of the program. Choose only a school that is accredited by the Accrediting Commission of Career Colleges and Schools or Technology. Have the school tell you in writing that it is accredited. You should be able to get a list of all the licensed private career schools in your state from your state education agency in the state capital.

Most grants, loans, and scholarships that are available to college students can be used for technical, trade, and business career schools as well. Some of these schools also offer their own limited scholarships, usually based on aptitude. Keep in mind that private career schools are generally more expensive than community colleges and their courses usually do not transfer for college credit. However, if a school gives you intense skills training and long-term assistance in finding a job, it may make good economic sense. Students who are able to move quickly into satisfying jobs can repay the cost of their education from their salary.

If you finance school with a loan, learn the terms of repayment. If you are offered financial aid, find out if it is a grant — a gift to you — or a loan that you must pay back. Make sure you understand when payback starts, how long you have to pay the loan back, and what the interest is over time. Call the Better Business Bureau and ask if there have been complaints about the program you are considering.

While most of these schools do not have dormitories, many are prepared to help non-local students find convenient and affordable housing and even roommates. If a program interests you but is not located near where you live, don't hesitate to call the admissions director and discuss whether the school has nonlocal students. For example, the Ocean Corporation, which trains divers for underwater construction, attracts students from all over the country to Houston and is accustomed to helping students find suitable accommodations for the twenty-two-week program.

Job Training Partnership Act Programs If your family meets the low-income requirements for these federally funded programs, you may be eligible to receive free entry-level job training. These programs usually concentrate on short-term training for quick entry into the job market at the lower levels. Once on the job, you can decide to continue studying and developing additional skills.

In many locales, several different groups will hold contracts to develop job training programs for teens and adults. You may find that a community near you runs some of these programs. Read the bulletin boards at your high school to get a handle on what's going on in your community.

One example of where to find this kind of training is the nonprofit Center for Employment Training (CET), which has more than forty training centers around the country. CET trains youth and adults who need to overcome reading, math and language barriers before getting a job. Their courses emphasize hands-on, self-paced instruction for jobs in demand in the local area. They teach both the basic skills and job skills required to get and perform on the job. Their courses take an average of six months to complete. Students are assisted in a job search when they demonstrate that they have the required skills.

Most large cities and many counties have job training programs funded by the federal government and, sometimes, by business partnerships in that community. The status of federal funding is presently undergoing great changes, and the future of these programs is not yet clear. Talk with a school career counselor for current information or call the state employment office to ask which training programs may be available to you. You can also call 1-800-JOB-CORPS. Leave your home phone number and a counselor in your area will call you back.

On-the-Job Training Some people land a job after high school that provides on-the-job training opportunities that let you keep growing and learning. Again, *you* have to take the lead on this. Ask about training opportunities when you are interviewing. After you are settled in your job and show that you are a reliable and responsible employee, speak with your supervisor or boss about your desire to develop new skills. Offer to work a bit extra if staff members will take time to teach you new things. Make it clear that you are ready to learn more and show that you appreciate the time people spend teaching you. Learn on your own by looking, listening, practicing, and studying. Explore the possibilities of a special training program. If you have a job in a trade or crafts profession, find out if you can join an apprenticeship program or otherwise become certified for obtaining a recognized level of competency. Certainly, you don't want an employer to take advantage of you, but you should be amenable to performing tasks if you are going to benefit as much as the employer.

Apprenticeship programs are linked to on-the-job training. For example, the Independent Electrical Contractors in Houston run a program that can, over four years, earn you journeyman status. IEC will help those chosen for the program find a full-time electrician's job. Participants attend a four-hour class one night a week for thirty-nine weeks a year for four years and pay $600 per year. Those who are successful on the job and in their classes are accorded the advanced status of journeyman, which qualifies them for better jobs. Participants in this program begin working for about $6.50 per hour and are given a 5 percent pay increase every six months as long as they continue to progress satisfactorily. IEC and programs like it are looking for students. Be aware that these programs require an understanding of algebra and geometry concepts. When you start job hunting, look for employers that offer on-the-job training opportunities.

Military The military offers high school graduates excellent training opportunities. There are 250 different job specialties from which you can choose, and the military guarantees new recruits that, if they meet the job qualifications, they will be trained in their area of choice. While you are in training, you will be given meals, housing, thirty days of paid vacation, free medical and dental care, and the opportunity for a paid college education. The military has been downsizing in recent years, however, and the standards for entry have become tougher.

In 1995, the U.S. Army, Navy, Air Force, and Marine Corps collectively recruited 168,010 new enlistees. Ninety-six percent of them had high school diplomas. It is possible but difficult to be accepted with a GED. Seven out of ten of the new recruits scored above average on the Armed Forces Qualification Test (AFQT), and higher scores mean more training opportunities. Just over one in ten (11 percent) of the new recruits were women. The number of women in the military is increasing, as are the opportunities for women to be promoted.

Each branch of the service has its own recruiting office. Different branches may be offering different training opportunities when you are ready to apply, so you may want to talk with more than one recruiter. Get out the phone book that has business numbers. Look for pages at the front of the book that give government numbers. In the section on the federal government under the heading Department of Defense, you should find a listing for each branch of the service and a list of all the recruiting centers in your area.

If you want the opportunity to train in the military, remain drug free, avoid criminal activity, and keep yourself in good physical condition. All recruits must pass a physical exam as well as the AFQT, meet height and weight standards, and be free of any major physical problems. Most young men and women who apply unsuccessfully are rejected for medical or moral reasons.

Once you apply and are accepted into the military, you will receive a contract for training and an active duty date. You can decide to enlist from two to six years. You may find that the training you want will require your service for longer than two years. High school students who enlist during their junior year (you must be seventeen) and attend two months of basic training in the summer between junior and senior year will be paid more and given a wider choice of training options.

It is wise to spend time gathering lots of information before you make a career decision. You might talk with one or more recruiters and then decide against the military. Sometimes, after you have decided against it, you will find you are still being recruited. It may take a very firm *no* — and even some parental help — to deter an eager and determined recruiter who has decided you'd make a great service person. Even though you took the AFQT test or spent time learning what a branch of the service had to offer, you are in *no* way obligated to the recruiter.

What Do You Do If You Have No Idea What to Do?

O.K., it's senior year, and the time to make some decisions is *now*. Perhaps you are completely confused or paralyzed or both. You know you need to make a decision about what kind of work to choose — but you can't, for the life of you, figure out what to do.

First thing to get through your mind: doing nothing *is* a decision. You have decided to choose "drift" as your course of action. In some rare circumstances, drift is O.K. In general, it is a poor idea. If you cannot decide, here are three options. One takes money. One takes time and discipline. And one you can do this weekend.

The first approach is to find a career counselor who can help you develop a course of action.

The second approach follows the same tack, but it's do-it-yourself. Go to the library or a bookstore and look through the many books on the career planning shelves. *What Color Is Your Parachute?,* the bible of career self-planning manuals, has long been a popular book, but good new career books appear every year. Go to the biggest bookstore in your area, look at all the choices in the career planning section, and buy the one that most appeals to you.

Or, try the third approach: gather your parents, siblings, best friends, and close relatives to brainstorm this decision with you. Ask everyone to comment about the three questions below. Ask one of the group members to run this discussion while you listen. This person should explain that put-downs or rude comments won't help you and are out of order here.

Here are the questions to be discussed:

1. What do those who know you consider your natural talents, skills, and interests?
2. Looking at how you spend your free time and where you have met success, what kinds of activities seem well-suited to you?
3. What career options do these answers suggest that you pursue?

Let people discuss these three questions for about an hour and come up with a list of possibilities they think might suit you. At the end of the hour, you can state whether there is anything on the list that you want to reject without discussion. You can cross out up to three items. Then brainstorm as a group a list of possible actions that emerge from the good ideas on the list.

Maybe your list of actions will look like this:

1. Go to the technical college and get a certificate in computer maintenance.
2. Go to work at McDonald's with the idea of working up to a manager. Think of this as a career decision, not a job.
3. Go to the community college and enroll in the computer graphics program.
4. Apply to the apprenticeship program for tile setters.
5. Apply to programs to study to be a chef.

Wildly different choices. Now, pick *one* — with the understanding that nobody is going to criticize you if it turns out not to be a happy choice. This is not a lifetime commitment. This is an I-will-try-this-on-for-size-for-at-least-fifteen-weeks commitment. Then go try it. It is better to try something and learn why it is not a good choice — or, if you're lucky, why it is — than to sit around waiting for the tooth fairy's twin sister to leave you the "perfect" career under your pillow. You may make a bad pick, and it may cost you some money — but don't consider it a mistake to try something and find out it isn't for you. Consider it a successful experiment because you gained *useful* information about yourself that you didn't have before.

It is important that I give you some information about the origin of this advice. I spent months talking with all kinds of "experts," asking them what to tell young people at the end of high school who found themselves clueless about their interests and abilities. There were no good answers. Finally I came to this conclusion: in the absence of a perfect plan of attack, settle for any plan of attack. Moving in the world is better than sitting on the couch. Working or learning anything is better than watching the soaps. It's better to *get started* than to sleep through the months after high school. You have lots of time to change your mind. *Now* is the time to begin something.

19. Which College?

Here's the deal: you get to make one of the most important decisions of your life in an area where you have no experience, little knowledge, and lots of confusing opinions. This has been known to put teens into a state of paralysis. Paralysis is a bad move.

First thing to do: relax. There are so many wonderful colleges and so many different ways to get a terrific education that the odds of choosing a place that will meet your needs are greatly in your favor. And there is so much help out there that if you stay open-minded, think broadly, put in a bit of effort, and, most importantly, read some of the millions of words written to help you, you are going to make an intelligent choice for yourself.

Think of it this way: you've just been invited to a fabulous buffet dinner. There are tables on the left with appetizers. Along the back are all kinds of salads. In the middle are tables with vegetarian dishes, beef dishes, and chicken dishes. And on the right are the desserts. You know there is no way you can taste everything. It would be a shame, though, to go to one table and taste only one dish and not taste anything else. You don't want to look at so many colleges that you get a stomach-ache — but be a little adventuresome in your search and go for a taste of something new.

Consider All of Your Options Think openly . . . be *open-minded*. Think *globally*. Don't consider only those colleges your friends are considering. Think about what *you* need and want. You can stay close to home or go to another part of the country. You can be part of a large university with big-time athletics and thousands of students or attend a small school and know most people in your class and all of your professors.

At college, you can study just about anything that interests you. There are university programs that teach you how to manage hotels, restaurants, arts groups, zoos, corporations, sports teams, construction projects, schools, or airports. You can learn interior design, landscape architecture, theater production, jewelry making, culinary arts, or graphic arts. Every kind of science from astronomy to zoology is available as a major. If you have a special interest, there is probably a college program that's just right for you.

You can be practical and career-directed or theoretical and liberal arts–oriented. There are colleges for people who like the outdoors and colleges for those who want to be in the center of major cities. You can go to schools where less then 20 percent of applicants are admitted or colleges where most all who apply have the chance to attend. You can pay $25,000 or you can pay $2,500 for a year's tuition. You can have a combined math and verbal SAT score of 700 or 1400.

Be realistic. About half the students who begin working toward a four-year degree do not complete their college education. Many who do graduate will not initially find jobs that require a college degree. Have contingency plans. Think about possible obstacles and how you can prepare to surmount them.

Use the Resources: You will find more books written about colleges and college admissions than you can carry home with you. For example, *Peterson's Guide to Four-Year Colleges,* which weighs over five pounds and costs $19.95, describes more than 1,600 colleges and universities and also lists them by cost, location, degree of admissions difficulty, and majors offered. There are guides to the most competitive colleges and guides to the best college buys. And then there are books — *Choosing a College* by Thomas Sowell and *Playing the Selective College Admissions Game* by Richard Moll, for example — that are full of realistic, sensible, insider advice. If you are aiming for the top of the top colleges, look for books like *Barron's Top 50,* which provides extensive, informal information about these highly competitive schools. If you are worried about money, look at *Cutting College Costs* by James Duffy.

Educational Strategies

There are many different ways to organize a college education. Start by thinking through which of the many options is going to suit you best.

Full-Time Student Living on Campus Live on a college campus, meet different kinds of people, get involved in college life, and have the time and freedom to explore new ideas, new ways of thinking, and new friendships. With this choice, you must make other choices. For example:

- *Serious scholar.* Aim for the highest level of academics you can manage without becoming overwhelmed. Focus on a four-year degree and on achieving the best academic record you can.

- *Focused career goal.* Look for a four-year college that is particularly good at teaching what you are interested in. Many colleges have a co-op program that alternates on-campus study with off-campus work.

- *Best financial deal.* Combine an interest in the quality of education with an interest in the best financial deal. Shop around for a good financial package that will help you pay for four years of school.

- *Small vs. big.* Some students love the diversity and activity of a large university. Others thrive in a smaller, more personal environment. Or spend two years at a small, personal college and do your last two years at a large university.

Full-Time or Part-Time Commuter Student Commute to school from home, either as a full-time student or as a part-time student combining school and work.

- *Community college first.* Start at a community college or junior college, improve your grades and academic skills, and transfer to a four-year college or university. (Check with the four-year colleges you are considering, however, to make sure they will accept your community college credits.)

- *Academically upwardly mobile.* Start at a local college, get great grades in hard courses, and work toward winning admittance and possibly a scholarship for your last two years at a more competitive college.

- *High-priced education, low-cost living.* Choose a private school that is more expensive than a public school but fits your needs and attend as a commuter to save on living costs, or get a live-in job with a family who will give you room and board.

Associate Degree Start out working toward a two-year associate degree without having to decide if you will continue on a for a four-year bachelor's degree. If you decide to continue, you can transfer to a four-year college and live on campus, commute while living at home, go full time, go part-time, go now, or take a break and go later.

Technical Certification Enroll in a college technical program to become certified or trained in a particular career area.

Defer and Take a Year Off Apply to college and be accepted while in high school but defer acceptance for a year. Spend the year doing something special — living in a foreign country, learning about what fascinates you, such as cars, sculpting, skiing, volunteering for a cause you care about — or gain work experience.

Do a Year of College Prep Do a "thirteenth" year of college prep work at a boarding school to beef up your academics in preparation for going to a more academically demanding college.

A Good Beginning If you're just starting to think about colleges and don't know much about the process, get yourself a copy of *The Complete Idiot's Guide to Getting into College* by Dr. O'Neal Turner. This easy-to-read book is $14.95 and well worth the money, considering that you may be spending several thousand dollars on your college decision. Perhaps your school will buy a copy. If you want to order it, tell your bookstore the ISBN number is 1-56761-508-2. It gives you all the questions you

Group Think

Try this: get together with a few good friends who are also thinking about college. The best time to do this is the spring of junior year or the summer before you are seniors. Buy *The Complete Idiot's Guide to Getting into College* — but don't buy one copy. Each of you should get your own. Read through it and write in it — ideas, notes about things to do, questions. Then talk about the questions and ideas in the book together. Help each other work through all the issues the book raises. If you do this right, you are each going to come up with a different list of colleges. If you already consider yourself sophisticated about college admissions, and you are interested in looking nationally, you may prefer the Sowell book, *Choosing a College.* If you are interested in the most competitive colleges, the Moll book, *Playing the Selective College Admissions Game*, is excellent. If you can't find these, look on the shelves at your bookstore or library and check with your school counselor. There are lots of good books available on college admissions.

If you can't seem to bring yourself to read anything about college, you may not be ready for college. After all, in college you'll be asked to read all the time.

should be asking yourself as you begin to consider which college is going to make you happy. It also gives you a practical time line and sensible advice about all aspects of going off to college.

What's Important?

What is important for you will be different from what is important for others in your class and maybe different from what your counselor values or, sometimes, what your parents value. But the considerations below apply for most everybody.

Good Advice

Stretch your brain. The more you learn at college, the better edge you have on life. All schools do not have the same standards. Work that might earn you an A at one college can be judged a C at a school with tougher standards. Aim high! **All other things being equal, you want to go to a college with academic standards that will stretch but not defeat you.**

Get an education even if you lack a career direction. If you already know what subject area interests you, look in the college guides that list the best programs by major. Choose schools that have well-developed programs. *But if you don't know what you want to study, don't worry.* It can be a mistake sometimes to force a career decision in high school when a few years of maturity and college exposure can guide you toward a better decision. Most teens go to college without a clear career direction and change their minds many times. Getting new ideas and reconsidering old ones is what college is about. Many famous colleges — schools like Harvard, Yale, Princeton, and Stanford — are liberal arts schools. Students at these schools choose "academic," not "career" majors. The purpose of liberal arts colleges is to teach you to think, write, organize, research, and wonder.

Find out what you don't know. You can't choose a school if you don't know it exists. **You won't choose a school you know nothing about** — even if it is perfect for you. Go looking for what you don't know. Starting in your junior year, sign up for college meetings at your high school. Go to the college fairs. Read through books like the *Princeton Review* and the *Fiske Guide*, which chat about schools.

Figure out what's going to work best for you. Think about big schools vs. small, city vs. small town, conservative vs. liberal, coed vs. single sex, fraternities and sororities vs. dormitories. You'll also want to think about religion, race, climate, and school character.

Don't confuse "doubt" with "don't." You don't have to be sure you want to go to a school to apply to it. **Only after you are accepted**

must you decide if it is the best school for you. But if you never apply, you will never get the chance to make that decision.

College is not a group decision. It is a really bad idea to choose a school based on where your friends are going. When you arrive at college to start freshman year, everyone is a beginner, everyone is looking for new friends, everyone is feeling a little scared. Choose the right place for your interests, your abilities and your desires, and making friends will be no problem. Don't be afraid to go it alone.

Say "later" to love. It is an equally bad idea to pick a school based on the wishes of your current boyfriend or girlfriend. Later on, when you marry, when you have children, when you are building your career, you will often need to put the needs of others first, to compromise and coordinate. **Now is the time to focus on developing you,** on getting a sound social, emotional, and intellectual foundation on which to establish that family and career.

An important part of college is developing independence. If you stay home, you can usually save money by living with your family. You may be able to continue in a job that you know and like to help with college costs. You will still be able to participate in family activities and have the support of your family and friends if you run into difficult patches. And your family can, in a small way, share in the flavor of your college experience. You will not have to go through an adjustment to a new place and a new way of living. Even if you stay in your hometown and live in a dorm, you can easily come home to do your laundry and mooch a good meal. This is a plus! *But . . .*

Going away and figuring out how to make it on your own is a great growing up experience. Living with other students can be noisy and crowded, but it also makes for wonderful times, deep friendships, stimulating conversations and profound revelations about the differences and similarities among us. The most enjoyable parts of college are often outside the classroom. If you are a commuter student who comes to class and leaves, you may miss an important part of the college experience. Tom Sowell writes in *Choosing a College*: "College is more than a preparation for a career. Often the person who graduates has become a different person from what he or she was as an entering freshman." This can scare parents, who may have little interest in seeing their carefully raised son or daughter develop a new set of values or beliefs, and it can cause tension for students. It can also be the most exhilarating, exciting, expanding experience of your life.

More expensive schools don't always cost you more. Regardless of what the school costs, you will be expected to make about the same contribution based on how much your parents earn and what assets you and your family own. There is a federal formula that is used to decide the general range of what is considered your fair share. Cost becomes a big factor for families that do not qualify for much aid but do not feel they can afford much tuition. Shop around for financial aid just the way you shop for colleges.

Don't let money stop you from going to college. Even if you are broke, *you can afford a college education*. Education in many states is a great bargain. Thousands of students live at home or with friends, go to school and work to pay tuition, books, and costs of living. If you must, you can take out a loan. Never pass up college because you think you can't afford it. This is a bad long-term economic decision. Go part-time so you can work more, take a year out before or during college to save or find a school with a great co-op program that arranges for you to alternate school and work. There are lots of choices available to you if you are willing to go looking.

Don't be passive. Jump in and listen, look, and ask. Talk with admissions or alumni representatives. Visit campuses, even if only locally. Read some of those books I mentioned earlier. Chat with lots of adults and college students. Again and again and again, teens tell me that they don't ask questions because they don't want to seem stupid or they don't know what to ask. *You have got to ask questions.* It is fine to say to an admissions person, "Look, I don't know anything about this school. I came because I am trying to figure out how I am going to decide and to find out about lots of schools. You must know a lot about this process. What do you think I should know about this school and about how to make a good decision?"

Remember, the college is selling itself and you are buying. You already know how to be a customer. All you have to do is get past any lack of confidence that keeps you from doing what you know how to do.

Kinds of Colleges

In addition to the generic considerations above, there are specific educational options that can narrow down your college choices:

- *Two-year, junior, or community college.* These are generally less expensive and sometimes less demanding initially than four-year colleges. Many two-year programs are designed to accommodate part-time students. You are likely to find few large lecture classes, no graduate teaching assistants and lots of academic support services. You can earn an associate degree in two years and, if you wish, transfer to a four-year program for a bachelor's degree.

- *Liberal arts college.* Here you will find an emphasis on general education in the humanities, social sciences, and physical sciences. Liberal arts schools such as Bates, Swarthmore, Carleton, and Pomona do not provide specific career preparation, but they include some of the most competitive, intellectually rigorous curriculums in the country. Many offer only undergraduate programs, but some, such as Harvard and Rice, are part of larger universities.

- *Comprehensive college.* Schools that offer both liberal arts and career-oriented courses are usually part of a university with graduate as well as undergraduate programs. The majority are part of large public universities. They offer students variety and diversity, but have more user-challenging administrations. Some state universities will have one large main campus and smaller branch campuses in other cities.

- *Military academy.* To apply to the United States military academies, students must be nominated by members of Congress. These schools award full scholarships in return for commitments to serve in the military. There are also tuition-based military academics, for example, Virginia Military Institute, to which students may apply directly.

- *Religious college.* These may be two- or four-year schools and may be liberal arts or comprehensive. Each will have a clearly defined religious orientation that influences the character of the college.

- *Specialization or pre-professional college.* These are schools that have chosen to specialize in the kinds of students they serve, for example, Spelman College which serves primarily African American women, or the particular area of study they teach as, for example, the Julliard School of Music. Students must have an interest in or aptitude for the school's specialization to attend.

- *Co-op college.* Hundreds of schools around the country have specially developed programs that coordinate working and studying into an integrated program. This helps students earn money as well as gain practical experience while going to college.

- *Single-sex college.* The student body is entirely or predominantly all men or all women.

On top of this, you will also want to consider whether you prefer city or country, big or small, close or far, private or public. You may be feeling confused by all these choices, but it's not as confusing as it may seem at first. Most students start out with preferences and limitations. In fact, college counselors most often find the hard part of helping students think through college options is not narrowing down the choices but encouraging students to think more broadly.

Your parents may be concerned about the cost of college or the distance from home. Find out what issues are important to them. Help them to think broadly, too. Don't rule out private schools, for example, based on cost, until you have done an accurate figuring for, say, the private university a few hours away. If you plan to have a car on campus that your parents are willing to fund, join a sorority or fraternity, or take more than four years to graduate because of scheduling difficulties and inaccessible advisers, the public university may turn out to be more expensive than your parents project. Go on a fact-finding mission, with your parents' help if they can offer it, before you start on the list-building phase discussed below.

Generate a List So, you've figured out what qualities you are looking for in a college. Now, find a computer program in your school or through some of the community-based youth groups that will help you search the entire database of colleges for the schools that fit your requirements. Ask your counselor if your school has such a program. Or call the public library. Many libraries now have college and career computer programs for public use. If you can't get access to the computer, never mind. Students have done this without computers for decades — and browsing through the college guide books may lead you accidentally to schools that might not have shown up on the computer list. By the start of your senior year, you want to have a list of possible colleges in hand. Some of you will have one sure choice. Those applying to competitive private colleges should consider five or six schools: one or two that are "reaches" — schools that interest you a great deal but which you are not sure will accept you; two or three that are "targets" — schools that fit your needs and where you fit the profile of students admitted and are likely to be accepted; and two "safeties" — schools you are quite sure will admit you. Every school will have an application fee so you are going to be spending a couple hundred dollars to apply (fees can be waived for income-eligible students) — but it makes sense in the context of spending thousands to attend.

It's Never Too Late If you are reading this in the middle of your senior year, you can still jump into the college game and play seriously. Many public universities have rolling admissions and accept students through

A Rejection Is Not a Statement About Who You Are

I know a terrific young man who was an outstanding student. He scored over 1300 on his SATs. He played the saxophone in the school band. He was the business manager for the school soccer team. He had a part-time job on weekends and somehow, in between, he volunteered to work with senior citizens. He applied early decision to Yale. And Yale rejected him. With letter in hand and despair in his voice, he asked his mother, "What else could I have done?"

For whatever reason, Yale decided it didn't need a sax-playing soccer manager that year. This was bad luck, not bad planning on his part. Yale was not rejecting him as a person but as a statistic in their charts. You cannot lead your life for some unknown college admissions officer who may or may not decide to put your application in the "yes" pile. Of course, pay attention to how the game is played. Know the rules of the game. Know the expectations. Talk with admissions people your junior year and ask for informal advice. And then do what you need to do for *you*.

This well-organized young man went on to lead a happy life absent Yale. His college rejection did not take away the pleasures and accomplishments of his high school years and the discipline he developed in his high school activities served him well as he moved into his adult life.

the spring. Some lesser known private universities don't fill all their slots and will also consider spring applications. Some schools have special programs for "late bloomers." You may be enrolled on a probationary status or required to take remedial or study skills classes, but you will have a chance to prove you can conquer college. The later you apply, the more difficult it will be to find housing and receive financial aid, so start right now getting a handle on which schools have good programs in your area of interest and which ones fit your needs.

The community college and junior college systems are wonderful places to regroup and recoup. No matter how poorly you did in high school, you can start over in the community college. If you get good grades in academic courses there, you can transfer to a four-year college. If you get great grades and show outstanding traits in a two-year college, you may find yourself with a slot at one of the top colleges in the country.

Financial Aid

The trail to financial aid is confusing and paper-laden. But there is so much written that if you spend an hour or two at the beginning of the process getting yourself straight on the way aid is organized, your task will be made easier. A good jumping-off point, again, is *Peterson's Guide to Four-Year Colleges*. In the blue pages at the start of the 1996 edition is a five-page piece by the director of undergraduate financial aid at Princeton University, "The Twenty Most-Asked Questions About Financial Aid." This is followed by a two-page chart to help you get an early fix on how much you will be expected to contribute to your college costs. There are many good books — *The Scholarship Book* by Daniel Cassidy or Peterson's *Winning Money for College* are two examples — that offer detailed financial aid information.

Need-Based vs. Merit-Based Aid Understand that most aid is "need based" rather than "merit based." This means that your family's financial circumstances determine how much you are offered. This is why it sometimes doesn't cost more to go to an expensive private school like Princeton, which charges $25,810 (1995 numbers) for tuition, room and board, than to the University of Texas (U.T.), which costs about $6,000, on the leanest budget, for tuition, room, and board. If, using the federal formula that all schools use, it is determined that your family can contribute $6,000 a year toward college costs, you are not likely to receive any aid for going to U.T. You should be able to get a financial aid package of nearly $20,000 from Princeton, based on "demonstrated need." The cost of the schools for you in this case is about equal.

But, if the formula says your family can contribute $12,000 per year, then it will cost you more than $12,000 in additional dollars to go to Princeton, and you can save more than $6,000 of what you are expected to contribute by going to U.T. over Princeton.

Demonstrated need is what the federal aid formula concludes your family can contribute. It happens sometimes that individual circumstances may make this formula look nuts to you. Say that based on last year's income tax, your family income was $50,000, but your dad's employer is closing his business and your father expects to be out of a job in thirty days. You will want to communicate any personal circumstances that are not clearly reflected on the financial aid application to the directors of financial aid at the schools you wish to attend.

Perhaps what the formula considers fair is not what your family is willing to pay. This is a discussion you must have with your parents before you start applying to schools. If your parents say, "Forget it, you're on your own," this doesn't mean their income doesn't count. Unless your parents do not claim you as a dependent on their income tax and you can prove you are self-supporting and completely independent of parents, you don't get more money because your parents can't or won't help. However, you can get student loans in your own name.

Financial aid packages have three parts: grants, which you do not have to pay back; loans, which you do have to pay back, usually starting six months after you stop being a full-time student; and work-study, which means you are guaranteed a campus job and the pay is calculated as part of your financial package. Schools can offer you identical amounts of aid, say, $5,000. But one school might give you a $2,000 grant, a $2,000 loan, and a $1,000 work-study commitment, while another school offers you a $500 grant, a $3,000 loan, and a $1,500 work-study commitment. With the second school, you are going to have to spend more hours in your work-study job and take on $1,000 more in debt. The first school is offering you a better deal — unless the second school is a much better academic institution for you and you're convinced you will get a better education and be a happier student there. Look, too, at what kind of loan a school is offering. There are all kinds of loans with different interest rates.

There is also merit-based aid, which is awarded based on your achievements, not your financial circumstances. The National Merit Finalist scholarships are examples of merit aid, as are athletic scholarships. Schools give merit-based aid to attract particularly able or gifted students, to diversify their student body, or to meet a certain campus need. Many communities offer a variety of scholarship awards, and many of these local grants are merit-based. Why not apply for all of those for which you are eligible?

Where's the Money? The largest amount of financial aid for colleges comes from the federal government's Pell Grants and from Stafford Loans and Parents Loans for Undergraduate Students (PLUS). The Pell Grants are outright grants for low income students and account for 18 percent of student aid. Stafford and PLUS loans provide 43 percent of all aid in the form of low interest loans. Of the 39 percent that comes from other sources, most of it is channeled through the financial aid office of colleges and universities. You can get direct grants yourself by winning essay contests, local scholarship competitions, and private awards, but there isn't a lot of untapped money floating around. More than 90 percent of all financial aid comes directly through colleges. Still, many able students win smaller scholarships that are offered by geography, place of parental employment, or interest. A one-time $500 award will buy books or clothes, and every penny helps.

Don't waste money on the for-profit companies that charge you $50 and $100 for scholarship lists. All of this information is available free. Many high schools purchase computer programs that allow you to search a data base for scholarship information applicable to your circumstances and/or provide monthly lists of opportunities for students in the school's geographic area. There are lots of books, too, that help you identify scholarship opportunities. If you do want to buy a list, go through a nonprofit company. The charge should be less than $20.

Your school's college counselor should have lists, updated throughout the year, of places to apply independently for aid. Of course, the more aggressive you are in applying, the greater the chance you have of finding what you want. If you choose to attend a public institution and live at home, an independent scholarship can be a great help because you may be able to cover most or all of your college costs without regard to your demonstrated need. If, however, you are going away to a private, expensive college that has calculated your need and determined how much money the college is going to award you in aid, a percentage of any scholarships you win independently will be deducted from the college's aid package. This is still an advantage because the money should be deducted first from the loan portion of your aid package rather than the grant portion.

First Step The very first step in the financial aid process, something you need to do wherever you go to school, is to fill out the Free Application for Federal Student Aid (FAFSA). Your school should have copies of this application. You cannot file a final version of this form before January 1 of the year for which you are requesting aid because the form asks for information from the just-completed tax year, but you want to file as soon after January 1 as you can. If your tax information for the previous year is not complete, you can use estimated numbers and file an update later. It takes about four to six weeks for the form to be processed, and then the government must send the financial analysis to the colleges you have indicated — who must get it before their financial aid cutoff date. You will get a copy, too, called a Student Aid Report. You or your parents should check it over to make sure it is correct. Depending on where you are applying, you may also need to fill out the College Board's Financial Aid Profile (FAF) and/or the Family Financial Statement (FFS). Individual colleges may have their own supplemental forms for you to fill out. Don't let the paperwork scare you. Just take the forms one at a time.

Ask Questions The most important advice I can give you is this: *don't be shy about asking questions*. Almost nobody understands all of this.

There are no dumb questions when you are tackling this for the first time. Financial aid officers expect you to call with questions and confusions, and you do not hurt your chances of getting admitted to college if you reveal that you are befuddled by the aid process. You may help your chances of getting money if you get good information and understand the process.

If your first choice college offers a smaller financial aid package than your second choice, call the financial aid director at the first college and negotiate before making any decisions. If you do get aid from a school but decide not to attend, tell them right away so the money can be available for someone else.

Your Getting-to-College Schedule

The best way to get ready to apply to colleges is step-by-step, year-by-year. If in the ninth grade you are determined to go to college after high school and you follow this schedule, it will lead you to the college door. If you are a junior or senior, begin with the eleventh-grade items and work your way through the list.

Ninth Grade

1. Have an academic plan. Make sure you are taking college-level courses. Get good grades. Take the hardest classes you can handle. If you are weak in an area, get help now and set yourself straight.
2. Start a college savings account. Save at least half of everything you earn if you can.
3. Read. Start building up your vocabulary now. Learn those vocabulary words in English class and use them when you talk.

Tenth Grade

1. Decide if you want to take the fall PSAT or PLAN. Use the
continued on next page

---

analysis that comes back with your scores to pinpoint your weak areas and focus on them.

2. If you are ready to think colleges, sit in on sessions with the college admissions people who visit your school. Start collecting impressions of colleges and narrowing down what you want.

3. Get involved in a school or community activity that appeals to you. Think about doing something interesting with the coming summer.

4. If you will need SAT II subject tests, which many of the most competitive colleges require, decide if any of them should be taken at the end of tenth grade when the subject is fresh in your mind.

5. Keep reading. Read any kind of books you like — but *read*.

6. Stay relaxed — but not so relaxed that you ignore thinking about life after high school. After the seniors get their college acceptances in April, schedule a visit with your school's college counselor. In the spring, review your classes, your GPA, and your plans for the future.

Eleventh Grade

1. This is the year to push for great grades. It is the last full year to build your transcript before applying to college. If you think you can take harder classes, do it. If you need help in any subject, get it right away.

2. Register for the fall PSAT.

3. Figure out when in the winter or spring you are going to take the SAT and/or ACT test. Get the registration book from your counselor's office and register early so you get the testing center you prefer. You may think you will not need one of these tests but change your mind later. Better to take it now. Again, think about SAT II subject tests. Decide what you need to take and when you will take it.

4. Start looking through books about colleges. Read the materials that may be coming to your house since you registered for college tests. Go to college fairs. Visit with at least three college

continued on next page

admissions officers who come to your school. Visit college campuses. Think about when you want to do this and start planning to visit somewhere. Go on a campus tour of the college nearest you. Use a computer program or a college guide to begin to focus on what you want in a college.

5. Decide if you want to take a special course to improve your college test scores this summer. Remember that scores seldom rise more than 50 points after prep courses.

6. Continue on with extracurricular activities you enjoy. Consider taking on a larger role in your activities. If you are working, save money for college.

7. Commit to having a "to consider" list of colleges ready by the start of senior year. Visit with your counselor to review your courses and activities and brainstorm about college possibilities. If you are considering an early decision application, you will want to visit colleges in your junior year or during the summer before senior year.

8. Read about financial aid in one of the guides. Sit down with your parents, get a fix on what your family is likely to be expected to contribute, and talk with your parents about whether they think this is realistic for them. Know, in general, what kind of financial help your parents think they can provide you. Use the financial aid section of any college computer programs in your high school or in the public library if one is available to help you estimate college costs and financial aid limits.

Twelfth Grade

1. Decide if you like your college test scores or if you want to take them again. If you are taking them again, register for the fall. If you have not taken the SAT or ACT, either register immediately or determine that the college that interests you does not require either.

2. Work on making your final choices. Get a plastic crate or file box to organize incoming material. Throw away what you are sure is of no interest. No later than October, you want to start writing

continued on next page

away for information and applications to the schools on your final list. You can do this with a plain postcard. *Make sure you know, in September, the application deadlines for admissions, housing, and financial aid for each school.* If you are applying to competitive public universities, it is wise to have applications in by Halloween. If you need financial aid, ask for forms from your colleges as well. Don't hesitate to call the financial aid officer and discuss what you should be doing to put yourself in the best position.

3. If you need financial aid, get a copy of the Free Application for Federal Student Aid from your counselor. Get your parents to begin pulling together the information they must provide. Submit the FAFSA as soon as possible. Make sure you check the deadlines for all schools of interest to you. For example, California public universities set a November 30 deadline for the FAFSA.

4. Decide if you want to apply "early decision" or "early action" to a college. You will only do this if there is a school you are sure is your first choice. Find out the deadline for early decision, which can be as early as November 1. The advantage of early decision is that you can know by Christmas if you are accepted, which makes for a very relaxed rest of your senior year. The disadvantage is that you have to make a decision about what school you most prefer before you may be ready.

5. Make a list of all the courses you have taken and will take by grade level. (Get a copy of your transcript to help you do this.) Make a list, also by grade level, of all outside activities in which you've been involved, either through school or in the community. You will use this in filling out your applications and in helping your references prepare their letters. Check to see if your school has a software program that helps you collect and organize this information.

6. Start working on those essays for your college applications if you are applying to schools that require them. You don't want to do them at the last minute, and you do want to get critiques

continued on next page

from teachers and adults who you think can help. The essays are important, so *spend time on them.*

7. After you send your application in, look at the scholarship opportunities your school college counselor should be posting every month. Decide whether you will apply and start in on completing the necessary forms.

8. If you have decided to attend a college in your local area — or at least for the first year — start gathering information now about your local choices, just as students who are looking out-of-town are doing. Don't assume that one particular school is where you will go because it is the school you know the most about. If you have a particular career area in mind, you will want to find out which college offers the best training.

9. If you are applying to the community college, you can apply as late as July — but earlier is better. If you want financial aid, apply by January 1 or earlier. Talk with the aid office about deadlines.

10. If your colleges request letters of reference, decide on whom you will ask and talk with those teachers. Don't wait until the last minute. Your teachers may have dozens of letters to write, and they may write a better letter if they have enough time. Give each reference a folder with a list of your courses and outside activities, your essay answers, the college form(s), a stamped envelope for each college, and a personal note of thanks.

11. If you are applying to several places, there is lots of paperwork. Stay cool. Stay organized. Start early. Make photocopies of every application *before* you start filling it in, in case you need a fresh copy, and *after* you have completed it, so you have a final copy.

12. Recognize that there are so many fabulous schools that life is not over if you don't get your first choice or even your second. Hope for and work for what you want, but don't let anyone convince you that your happiness depends entirely on getting into X school. Make sure you have applied to a safety school, a place where you and your counselor think you are highly likely to be admitted.

13. Pay attention to those first-semester grades. They count.

14. Get everything in and enjoy senior year.

20. Solving Personal Problems

Are you struggling with a problem that is weighing you down? Sometimes teens have problems related to family issues. Sometimes problems come from poor choices you have made in the past. And sometimes, problems just fall on you.

It really doesn't matter how a problem lands on your shoulders. What matters is that you face serious personal issues head-on. Allowing a problem to go unaddressed is like ignoring a slow leak in a tire. You may not realize how much the situation is slowing you down until it brings you to a complete stop. Worrying about health or family finances, alcohol or drugs, depression or despair, makes it hard to concentrate on schoolwork. If your parents are worrying, it can also affect you and get in your way of being focused on school. Sometimes parents benefit from getting help with their own problems, and you may be able to talk about this at home. But if your family's problems are out of your control, you must focus on what you can do for yourself.

If you are a teen and you know, even if you haven't admitted it to anyone, that you have a problem with drugs or alcohol, eating disorders or depression, *now* is the time to get help. An addiction is difficult to break, no matter how much you want to shake it. Working with others who understand the issues you face and have experience addressing your kind of problem often makes the difference — both for the person who is addicted and the family who wants to support that person.

Some problems are physical. You may not know that you need glasses, a hearing device, dental work, or other medical attention until you visit your doctor. Physical pain or difficulty is the body's way of saying to the brain, "Pay attention to me." Never feel embarrassed about describing your difficulties and asking for help. Take a persistent physical problem seriously. If money is an obstacle, talk to your doctor about this. Many health care providers will work with you to solve your problems, both financial and physical. If the first person you ask for help cannot help you, try someone else. Your school nurse or counselor may be able to connect you with services for a small fee or for no cost.

Some problems are emotional, and they should be regarded with the same seriousness as a physical illness. In fact, emotional problems can occur for physical reasons. Depression is often as physically based as a broken bone and needs to be treated with the help of trained professionals. Teen bodies are filled with hormones that fluctuate a lot. Don't ignore the power of hormones to create emotional havoc.

When one person in your family is undergoing serious difficulty, it is almost always the case that other people in the family are affected in some way. For that reason, it is best to have the truth out on the table so everyone can understand what is going on rather than feeling mysterious vibrations that float around in the air. Most of the time, the right thing to do is for you to talk with a parent first about what is troubling you and together look for solutions. If you are a teenager who feels you just can't, right now, talk with a parent, look for an adult you trust and open up to that person about your need for assistance.

I wish I could promise you that if you reach out for help, every problem will instantly be fixed. You know that isn't true. What *is* true is that most problems teenagers describe as hopeless can, in fact, be made better. It is always worth trying. Let your counselors, teachers, or others in your school who are there to connect students with community resources help you.

Many teens — and adults — fail to see that our minds and our bodies are connected. Stress and worry can cause you real physical symptoms, such as stomach pain, headaches, fatigue, floating pains. One way for you to combat stress is to talk through problems with a wise and sympathetic adult. Reading a book about an issue that is troubling you is another way to get help — just go browsing at your largest bookstore. Joining a support group can also help.

Many communities publish a directory of services that are available locally. The United Way, any agency with the words "family" and "children" in its title, the public library, or the school counseling office may have such a book. For direct access to city, county and federal resources, look in the government pages in the front of the phone book. If you have separate business and residential phone books, this information is usually in the front of the business phone book, sometimes printed on blue paper.

If you have access to the Internet, there are all kinds of resources available to you for all kinds of problems. Some links connect you with support groups, others with professionals. Often you will find people on the net who have the same problem as you do talking about how they cope. One excellent resource is the American Self-Help Clearinghouse which can be found on the Internet at http://www.cmhc.com/selfhelp/.

Here are some national resources for specific problems that you can call both for general information and connections to local resources:

AIDS If you are worried about AIDS, get yourself tested. Most urban communities have a clinic that provides free or low-cost testing and counseling. For information, call the Teen AIDS hotline 1-800-234-8336 (4 to 8 P.M. Eastern Standard Time, Monday through Friday). For HIV information, call the HIV Hotline, 1-800-342-2437. This line should answer twenty-four hours every day. Most importantly, you should know that HIV is no longer a death sentence, especially if you get early treatment and support. But you should also know that every sexually active individual *must* be well informed about AIDS prevention. This is a disease that can strike anyone, man or woman, hetero- or homosexual if you do not become informed and take correct precautions. Call your local health department for AIDS prevention information.

Abuse If you are being abused sexually, physically or emotionally, you MUST find an adult who can help you. Go to a place of worship — even if you don't belong. Walk in and ask to speak to a spiritual leader. Or go to a hospital and ask to speak to a social worker. Go to school and talk privately with the principal or the head counselor. Talk to a teacher or trusted adult. If you need help immediately, call the county Child Protective Services or call the local police and ask to speak to someone familiar with issues of abuse. Many police departments now have people specially trained to talk with you about physical or sexual abuse. Or call the juvenile division of your sheriff's office or county police force.

There is nothing you have done that means you deserve to be beaten or repeatedly humiliated or used sexually against your will. For a local referral, call the National Committee to Prevent Child Abuse, 1-800-CHILDREN.

Drugs There are lots of different groups helping to fight drug addiction. Sometimes it takes a while to connect with the one that can help you. Usually, there is an umbrella agency to which all the different groups in an area belong. If you can't find that number locally, call the Hotline for Alcohol and Drug Abuse, 1-800-777-2721. Explain your problem and your age and ask where you can go for help. It is impossible to move forward with your life if you are addicted to drugs. Breaking an addiction is difficult but thousands of young people have done it successfully and so can you — but it almost always requires help.

Alcohol One place to call if you are drinking too much is Alcoholics Anonymous (AA) which should have a listing in your local phone book. You will find people who share and understand your problem. Call any time of the day or night. Someone will talk with you about what is going on that minute, and they will tell you where the nearest AA group is for you to attend later. Then get yourself there. No one will ask your last name, your address or phone number. Everything you say will be confidential.

If your parents or friends drink to excess, by all means join Alateen, an Alcoholics Anonymous support group for teens. The national number for information and pamphlets is 1-800-356-9996. For meeting information, call 1-800-344-2666.

Food If you are binge eating and throwing up or not eating at all, you are in danger of doing long-term, serious harm to your body. This is not a problem you should ignore. Get help immediately so you can figure out how to stop this dangerous pattern. Here are two national groups focused on eating disorders: National Association of Anorexia Nervosa and Associated Disorders (ANA), P.O. Box 7, Highland Park, IL 60035; (708) 831-3438; and the American Anorexia/Bulimia Association, Inc. (AABA), 425 E. 61st St., 6th floor, New York, NY 10024; (212) 891-8686.

If you believe food is your addiction, look for a local chapter of Overeaters' Anonymous.

Smoking If you want to stop smoking, consider finding a support group. You might discuss a nicotine patch with your family doctor. For advice on how to stop smoking and an explanation of what smoking does to your body, call your local chapter of the American Heart Association, the American Lung Association, or the American Cancer Society.

It is difficult to stop smoking because the nicotine in cigarettes is addictive. If you are only smoking a small amount, stop now before the addiction increases. If you haven't started, don't! Not smoking is one of the most important things you can do for your long-term health.

Grief If someone you love has died and you are feeling pain from your grief, it can help you a great deal to talk with someone who understands the grieving process. Research studies show that this is a very important way to help people who are suffering from loss. Even if you don't belong to a religious group, you might want to visit with a minister, rabbi or priest. You can also call a crisis hotline in your community to find support groups. Go to the library or bookstore and look for a book that can help you.

Rainbows International has 6,300 affiliated groups around the country. Rainbows establishes peer support groups in churches, schools, or social agencies for children and adults who are grieving a death, divorce or other painful transition in their family. Groups are led by trained adults and there is both a secular and religious version of their program. There is a special program, "Spectrum," for teens dealing with death or divorce, and Rainbows will offer help in forming small, local support groups. Rainbows, 1111 Tower Rd., Schaumburg, IL 60173. Call (847) 310-1880 or 1-800-266-3206; fax: (847) 310-0120.

Overall Health If you have a physical problem that has bothered you for a while, now is the time to take care of it. Talk with family, talk with your doctor by phone, talk with the school nurse. Your county chapter of the American Medical Society can help with referrals. Planned Parenthood offers clinics for female health issues. They charge on a sliding scale that adjusts the fee to your family income.

Most chronic illnesses have national family support and/or information groups. It can be very helpful to connect with other people informed in the area of concern to you. Ask your physician if he can connect you with the right group. For example, you can call the Cancer Information Center, 1-800-4-CANCER or the American Cancer Society, 1-800-227-2345 for cancer-related information. Parents who need help providing acute medical services to children can call the National Children's Cancer Society, 1-800-5-FAMILY.

Teeth If you have a dental problem, you want to get it fixed. Bad teeth don't cure themselves; they just become a more serious problem later. Losing teeth when you are older will not be fun, so cure your toothaches now. If lack of money is stopping you, look for a dental school that offers services at a reduced fee. You can also explain the situation to your dentist or talk with the local chapter of the American Dental Society.

Suicide No matter how bad things look today, how much you believe the pain will never go away, no matter how much shame or despair or fear you may feel, suicide is *not* the answer to your problem. Suicide fills the world with more pain. Call your local information and ask if there is a Crisis Hotline in your community; call the Covenant House Hotline, which is open twenty-four hours a day, 1-800-999-9999; or call the Boys Town National Hotline, 1-800-448-3000.

For information and referrals on dealing with problems related to suicide, call the American Suicide Foundation. If you want to talk with an adult at school, help them understand that this is an emergency so that they don't mistakenly put you off without understanding the depth of your sadness.

Runaways Call Covenant House, 1-800-999-9999 or the National Runaway Hotline, 1-800-392-3352. If you are thinking of running away, instead run toward someone who can give you support right in your community.

Learning Disabilities See Chapter 15; contact the Learning Disability Association of America, 4156 Library Rd., Pittsburgh, PA 15234. Call (412) 341-1515. Fax: (412) 344-0224

Gangs I list gangs along with other health problems because being part of a gang can be a serious health problem. Maybe you worry about acne, weight, bad hair, or crooked teeth. These don't compare to a bullet in your body. Yes, it makes sense to want to be part of a group where you feel welcomed and valued. It feels good to have pals you can trust. But it is absolutely crazy to try to get these good feelings by hanging out with a group of people who are likely to lead you to jail, trouble, violence, and fear. Stay away, *far* away, from guns. Guns are not a symbol of power. Guns are a symbol of fear.

There are better groups to belong to. This book is full of suggestions about how to join up with many different kinds of people who are ready to make you part of their world. Your life is valuable and you are a valuable resource for your community.

The community needs you to be a success, not a statistic. If you need help with a gang-related problem, call the local anti-gang task force hotline. Most big cities have one. If your community does not, then talk with your counselor, with a police officer or with a trusted teacher. It is normal to think that the adults in your life simply don't understand what is going on with you. But, honestly, do you think every adult you know has forgotten their teenage years? Adults *can* understand, and they *can* help if you decide help and support is what you want.

Personal Perversity What kind of problem is this, you may be asking. Personal perversity is an affliction that can make you as unhappy as a toothache or a chronic illness. Sometimes, people don't learn the emotional skills they need to get along well with others in the world. Without them, you are as likely to suffer pain and discomfort as people with physical problems. Like physical problems, these emotional problems can be treated. You can learn interpersonal skills that will make you happier and healthier. Sometimes you need a therapist, but sometimes you just need a coach who can show you different ways to approach problems and people. If you get "pissed off" easily, if you find you are mad more than you are relaxed, if you are easily moved to anger or tears or frustration, you may be suffering from personal perversity. Now, during your teen years, is the best time to make some small changes in approach and outlook that will pay off handsomely in the years ahead. Disagreeable perversity is a kind of vinegar that adds a sour taste to whatever it enters. Like vinegar, it should only be used in very small amounts. You don't want a daily glass of it.

Ask for Help

It is easier to deal with difficult problems when there is someone there to assist us. It is neither necessary nor wise to handle difficult physical or emotional problems alone. It's a sign of strength and maturity to recognize a serious problem and figure out where and how to find help. Every community is full of adults who want to help teenagers. Many adults were themselves helped along the way and would be pleased to show thanks by returning the favor.

Sometimes your parents want to help you but they're in over their heads. Maybe they have no experience with the problem you bring to them. Maybe your problem scares them. Maybe they feel guilty because they wanted to protect you from painful situations. Maybe you are so good at hiding the truth that they don't realize how much you need help. I think it used to be easier for parents to figure out how to approach problems when families lived near each other or parents had time to sit in the park or on the school grounds with other parents and talk.

Today, many parents are pressured by their responsibilities and can't find the time to make personal connections, to give advice and comfort and to find laughter. It is very important that parents *make* the time to find people who understand and can talk about the tensions and difficulties your family faces. If you think this would be a good idea for your parents, speak up. Maybe you can say to your family, "I feel confused about what to do and maybe you do too. I think it would be worth a try to see if we couldn't find some outside contacts that can help us deal with this." If your family is unable to help you, then you must go it alone and figure out how to find responsible resources in your school or your community that will help you. Use the suggestions in these pages to get started.

Every community needs for its young men and women to do well. Each of us gains every time one teenager recovers from difficulty. When our teenagers are healthy and happy, we are a healthier, happier nation with a brighter future.

21. In Closing

Look in the mirror. I don't know what you see, but I'll bet it is different than what I would see if we were standing side by side. Maybe you are focusing on your hair or your chest or your teeth. I, after living with this book for more than a year, would be seeing your possibilities. As a teenager, you are standing in front of the door to adulthood. You are a blackboard with the word "opportunity" written across it. You are energy, ideas — and probably confusions. You are this terrific work-in-progress, and I am rooting hard for the finished product to be a work of art. But I know that you have difficult decisions to make, dangerous temptations to resist, demanding tasks to conquer. I hope *The Real High School Handbook* will help you choose wisely and move forward happily.

Every teenager really is special. Every school district is different. Every family is unique. Getting ready for your life is not an assembly-line operation. It is hand-crafted work, and no two products are ever alike. This book is not about finding the *right* answer, because there isn't one right answer. It is about providing you and your family with the right information so you can collaborate in making good, personal choices.

Use this book to help you ask questions and get answers. Use it to develop a plan for your high school years so at the end you arrive at a place you want to be. Use it to figure out your choices. And use it to open lines of communication with parents and teachers. Do everything with this book you cannot do to textbooks. Underline, make notes to yourself, tear out pages, turn down corners. Make this book yours; let it help you survive and thrive in high school.

I have worked hard to verify all the information in these pages, but, please, double check with your school or with any programs that interest you to make sure you have the most current and accurate details. I have also asked experts from around the country to review various chapters and add their perspectives, and they have made terrifically helpful contributions; but in the end this book reflects my experiences and values. It was, in fact, my experiences as a high school student mentor that motivated me to write this book.

I wished all the teens I met could have wise and involved parents, experienced and caring counselors and savvy mentors follow them through all four years of high school. I can't make that happen. Instead I have tried to put in your hands just the sort of advice and encouragement you would get from such people. Now, no matter your circumstance, you have the information to take charge of your high school years and graduate well-prepared for life.

If sections of this book are especially helpful to you, I would love to hear from you. If you uncover errors, disagree with points of view or have comments, please let me hear about those as well. If you just feel like writing to tell me about how high school is for you, I hope you will do it.

In case you still haven't gotten the message of this book firmly in hand, here's one last blast: Figure out what you want and need from these years in high school to help you be a happy, productive adult. Don't drift. There are lots of choices — but you have to make them and make them wisely. Do whatever it takes to make your life work. *Do it. Do it now!*

Do well. Be well. Have fun. Keep that stress in check and take pleasure in what is a hard but exciting time in your life. Every day is a new day, and every day something good can happen — especially if you are helping happiness along.

22. For Parents

Stay in the Loop

The Real High School Handbook is addressed to teens, but it's intended for parents as well. The message, as you will see in the first two chapters, Master of Your Fate, Captain of Your Soul and What Attitude Are You Wearing?, is that teenagers should be captain of their own team. They must take charge of the high school process and not rely on others to provide the "right" answers. But that doesn't mean teens are ready to be set adrift to manage on their own.

In her insightful book *In the Shelter of Each Other,* Dr. Mary Pipher observes that teenagers today very much need parents to help them "reject what is hurtful and select what is helpful." She despairs that "in our culture, after a certain age, children no longer have permission to love their parents. We define adulthood as breaking away, disagreeing and making up new rules. Just when teenagers most need their parents, they are encouraged to distance from them."

High schools can be inhospitable to our inquiries and work pressures can get in the way of our decoding the complexities of high school in the 1990s. *Resist!* This book will help you to stay involved by giving you the background information you need and a structured way to talk with your teenager about school issues.

Coach for Success

Teenagers need parents. Teens need our cheers when they are doing well. They need optimism and support when they are falling apart. They always need love and concern. They don't always make it easy for us to be loving, but our job as parents is to hang in there through the good times and the bad and not give up — or give out.

When my teenage sons harassed me for some parental failing, I would remind them that the advantage of not having perfect parents is that they needn't be perfect kids. We all make mistakes. Like growing up, parenting is complicated and confusing. Parents sometimes report that they hold back talking with teens because they are unsure of what to say. It's all right to say, "Look, I am not sure what the right thing to do here is. Let's see if together we can figure it out." When you're mired in a bad patch of adolescence, it's also okay to say. "Whatever is going on between us feels bad, and this tension isn't good for our family. Help me to figure out how I can help you. I can't stop caring and feeling concerned, but I can try to see things through your eyes if you will talk with me."

These kinds of confusions occur all through adolescence, but they often are exacerbated by moving from middle school to high school. Chapter 3, For Ninth Graders Only, focuses on this transition into high school. Chapter 20, Solving Personal Problems, offers both teens and parents resources for addressing persistent problems.

Ask Questions

High school today is not the same as it was when we were there. Chapter 4, The Rules and Requirements, and Chapter 6, How Do You Choose Courses?, can help bring you up-to-date. Chapter 7, Subject by Subject, explains the rationale for required courses. For more information, read Chapters 5, 8, and 9. All these chapters will, I hope, stimulate family discussion.

Throughout *The Real High School Handbook*, teens are urged to keep asking questions until they have the answers they need. I urge the same of parents. Stay in the loop. Your asking questions may help your teenager become more comfortable asking questions, too.

If each student is captain of his own team, teachers and parents are coaches. Think about the role of good coaches on winning teams. They make sure the players show up for practice, learn the drills, master the techniques and keep a positive attitude. They set rules and expect them to be followed. They insist their players eat nutritiously and sleep sufficiently. Always, they focus on success. Chapter 2, What Attitude Are You Wearing?, points out that success in academics is much like success in sports. Keep practicing, put in the time, keep a positive attitude, and success is likely.

Every spring, have a "formal review" with your teenager. Go over a current transcript together and review a course planner. Talk about goals for the coming year. Chapter 16, Extracurricular Activities, reports on research that says students who are involved in an extracurricular activity at least one hour a week are more likely to be successful. Talk about what activities may work well for your teenager. Parents can't decide what teenagers should be interested in nor force teens to do things they strongly oppose, but they can suggest, encourage and support.

When you and your child are reviewing, talk about summer plans. Summer's a good time to work on problems that are getting in the way of school success. But it is also a wonderful time to build on strengths. Chapter 10, What Does It Mean to Be "Smart" and How Do You Get Smarter?, discusses different kinds of intelligence. Help your teenager find ways to exercise his or her best talents. For all of us, successes build our self-esteem and help us struggle through the hard parts of life.

Define the Problem

Failures are toxic. Every now and then a reminder from the world that there is no free lunch can be instructive, but a continuing lack of success is discouraging and dispiriting. If your teenager is consistently unhappy in school and/or repeatedly doing poorly, you must jump in to help. Chapter 11 offers suggestions on what to do when classes are not going well. Chapter 14 talks about Different Ways to Do High School and Chapter 20, Solving Personal Problems, is full of resource referrals. If your instincts tell you that something is awry with your teenager, trust those instincts. It may be normal adolescence causing temporary turbulence, or there could be a real problem that needs your attention.

Defining and diagnosing problems can be perplexing. Listen carefully and thoughtfully to what counselors and teachers have to say, but trust your own judgment — and your child's judgment. If what you are hearing doesn't feel right, look for a second opinion. There are many parent support groups which offer information and advice at no cost. Chapter 15 offers more complete discussion of diagnosing learning problems.

Of course, teenagers need to move out into the world, try on ideas and experiences different from ours, make mistakes and deal with the consequences. When we try to caution them, they tend to think that either we never were teens or that we lost the part of our brain that recalls those years — or that being a teenager in such a distant past bears no resemblance to being a teenager today. We may not convince them differently, but we can think back to those years, to how we felt and what we did and what we wished our parents would have done. Remembering my own adolescent need for independence helped curb my inclination to worry all the time and be too rigid with rules and restrictions for my own sons. Many of the arguments between parents and teens are really about power, control, and autonomy, not curfews, homework, and money. It may help to address these larger issues head on. Speaking to an outside person — a counselor, a therapist, a trusted friend, or a relative — can help put issues in perspective.

This book frequently suggests teens check in with their counselor. Parents play a role different than teachers and counselors who have many students to advise and must be fair and equitable for all children in the district. A parent advocates for only one child at a time. Every student needs an advocate — someone whose primary interest is one personality, not a class or a school or a district. Parents who are rude and annoying don't help their children, but sometimes it does take a parental "squeaky wheel" to move things in the right direction.

Understanding the Changing World of Work

One of the things that has changed dramatically from our high school years is the world of work. Chapter 13, Getting Real About the World of Work, gives you some statistics about education and employment and a great deal to discuss with your teenager at the kitchen table. There are four other chapters in this book that are intended to help teens prepare for the transition from school to work. Chapters 12 and 14 discuss using high school classes to investigate careers and develop workplace skills. Chapter 17, Why College?, helps students decide if they want to go immediately from high school to college. Questions in this chapter can help open a discussion between parents and teens. About three quarters of all high school students say they want a four-year college degree but only about 30 percent receive it. It is important that teenagers look realistically at all their options and opportunities. If your son or daughter is not unquestionably college-bound, you can help by encouraging him or her to spend time on researching all the options. These options are summarized in Chapter 18.

If your child is headed to college, Chapter 19 provides a year-by-year schedule of things to do to prepare for college. Also, Chapter 9 includes a section specifically on college admissions tests.

To All Good Things

There are no "right" answers. Every teenager really is unique. Getting ready for life is custom-crafted work, not assembly-line production. Our teenagers are works-in-progress. The intent of *The Real High School Handbook* is to help teens — and parents — find the information they need to put in place a good foundation. Good questions lead to good answers, and good answers lead to good choices. May *The Real High School Handbook* lead you and your teen to good conversations, good decisions, good times, and good fortune. Good luck.

Index